Fourth Edition

bju **press**®

Greenville, South Carolina

Note: The fact that materials produced by other publishers may be referred to in this volume does not constitute an endorsement of the content or theological position of materials produced by such publishers. Any references and ancillary materials are listed as an aid to the student or the teacher and in an attempt to maintain the accepted academic standards of the publishing industry.

SCIENCE 2
Fourth Edition

Writers
Peggy S. Alier, MEd
Debra Harrold White

Contributing Writers
Betty Doeppers
Joyce Garland, MEd
Janet E. Snow, MA
Bethany Wilkison

Bible Integration
Wesley Barley, MDiv

Project Editor
Kristin McClanahan

Page Layout
Faith Bupe Mazunda

Concept Designer
Drew Fields

Designer
Josh Frederick

Project Coordinators
Nathan Doney
Gina Stewart

Consultants
Brad Batdorf, PhD
L. Michelle Rosier

Cover Designer
Drew Fields

Permissions
Tatiana Bento
Sylvia Gass
Kathleen Thompson
Carrie Walker

Illustrators
Cynthia Long
Craig Oesterling
Kathy Pflug
Lynda Slattery
Courtney Godbey Wise

Art Liason Facilitators
Jim Fraiser
Julia Young

Photo credits appear on pages 205–6.

© 2017 BJU Press
Greenville, South Carolina 29609
First Edition © 1975 BJU Press
Second Edition © 1989, 1998, 2003 BJU Press
Third Edition © 2010 BJU Press

Printed in the United States of America
All rights reserved

ISBN 978-1-62856-048-0

15 14 13 12 11 10 9 8 7 6 5 4 3 2 1

Contents

God's world is full of amazing things. They are all around you. You are studying science to learn about God's world. The way people think about the world is called their worldview. The following points are from a Christian worldview. They can help you understand science.

1. God is the Creator.

God created all things in just six days! God made everything perfect (Genesis 1:31). You see many things as you learn about the world. You see God's power. You see His goodness. You see His wisdom. Learning about God's creation makes us want to praise Him.

2. The Fall changed God's world.

God's world is not perfect now. Adam disobeyed God. Because of Adam's sin, the world changed (Genesis 3:17). Thorns grow from the ground. Work is hard. Living things die. But using science helps people live and work in this imperfect world.

3. God has provided redemption.

Sin has affected God's world. But God still loves and cares for His world. He sent His own Son Jesus into the world. Jesus saves all people who believe the gospel. One day God will make the world perfect again. Until then, Christians should live to glorify God.

4. People are important.

You are made in God's image (Genesis 1:26). People around you are too. God wants you to show His love to other people (Matthew 22:39). Science can be used to help or to hurt. You should use science to show love to other people.

5. God created people to work.

God wants people to use His world wisely. He wants people to work to make it better (Genesis 1:28). Work is good. God gave people the job of managing and caring for the plants and animals. Learning things about our world helps you honor God in your work.

These points can help you serve God with science. Think about them as you read!

1

What Scientists Do

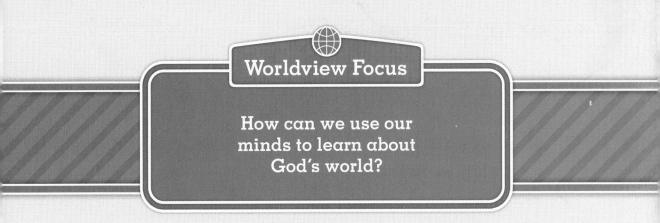

Science is the study of the world around us. The world is God's world. It shows what a great God He is. It is a world full of new things.

God gave people minds to learn. He is pleased when we use our minds to learn about His world.

Scientists study God's world. They use skills and tools to help them. They do tests to solve problems. You can be like a scientist as you use your mind to learn.

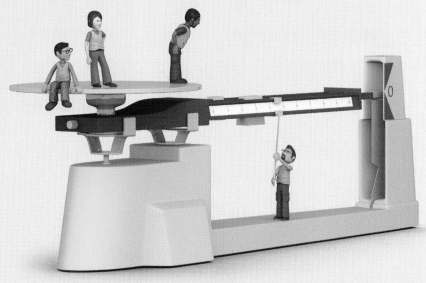

Science Process Skills

Scientists use their minds to discover things about God's world. They learn about what they see. They try to solve problems. Scientists use skills to help them gather and use information as they study the world. These skills are called **science process skills**. Christians can use their minds to solve problems and study God's world.

Observe

You observe to find out about things. You see, hear, taste, smell, and touch. You use your senses to observe.

 Why do we use science process skills?

Classify

You classify when you group things. You can group things by kind or size. You can group things by color or shape.

Measure

You measure to find out how much. You can find out how many or how heavy. You can find out how big or how long. You can find out how hot or how cold.

Infer

You infer when you use what you know to tell why things happen. You know that some hot things make steam. You can infer that a pot that is steaming is hot.

Why do we measure?

Predict

You predict when you use what you know to say what may happen. You know that sunlight is warm. You can predict that ice in sunlight will melt more quickly than ice that is away from sunlight.

Communicate

You communicate when you share what you know. You may tell others or show them.

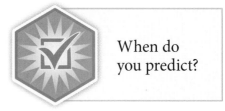

When do you predict?

Science Tools

Scientists use tools to find out things. Tools help them observe and measure things. You can also use science tools to help you observe and measure.

Hand Lens

You use a hand lens to observe small things. A hand lens helps to make things look bigger. Moving the lens can help an object look larger and clearer.

 Why do we use science tools?

Ruler

You use a ruler to measure how long something is. Scientists use the metric system for measuring. They measure centimeters with a ruler.

Measuring Cup

You use a measuring cup to measure volume. Volume is how much space something takes up. Beakers are measuring cups that scientists use to measure milliliters.

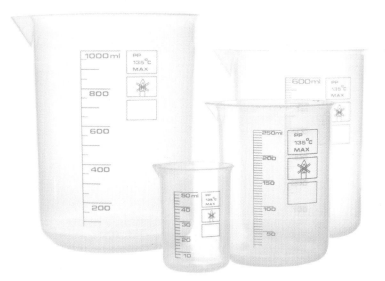

Balance

You use a balance to measure how much matter is in something. Scientists use a balance to measure with grams. Matter is anything that takes up space. A rock is matter. A flower is matter. You are matter!

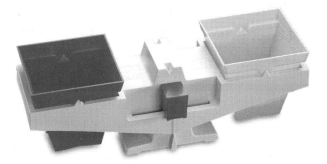

Thermometer

You use a thermometer to measure temperature. A thermometer tells how hot or cold something is. Scientists use Celsius thermometers.

What are beakers?

A Science Experiment

Scientists study the world around them. They try to answer questions. They try to solve problems. They use experiments to do these things. An **experiment** is a scientific test to solve a problem. The test is the **process,** or steps, the scientist will follow.

A scientist does experiments to find things out. You can also do experiments.

Ask a Question

You ask a question if you want an answer to a problem. Decide what you want to know and write a question about it.

Form a Hypothesis

Write a hypothesis. A hypothesis is a possible answer to a question. You write it as a statement you can test.

Plan Your Test

Decide how to test your hypothesis. Think about the steps, or procedure, of your test. Think about the things you will need to do your test. Think about how you will make the test fair. You must test the same things to have a fair test.

Which cups would make a fair test?

What do scientists use to answer questions?

Do Your Test

Follow your procedure. Observe what happens. Then write down or draw what you observe. You can make charts, lists, or pictures to record information.

Draw Conclusions

Conclusions are the ending ideas. Think about what happened. The test results might agree with your hypothesis. But they might not. You might have learned something new. You should be able to apply what you learned.

Communicate

Share what you learned with others. You could use a written report. You could tell them. You could use a graph or picture.

 What are some ways to record information?

ACTIVITY

Keeping Cool

A car sitting in the sun gets hot inside. Some adults say a light-colored car can feel cooler. You can do a test to find out. You cannot test cars, but you can test colored paper.

Problem

Does color affect temperature?

Materials
black paper
white paper
tape
2 thermometers
Activity Manual

Procedure

1. Fold the black paper in half. Tape the long edge and one short edge to make a sleeve as shown in the picture.

2. Fold and tape the white paper the same way.

3. Place one thermometer in each paper sleeve.

4. Look at your paper sleeves. Think about the problem question.

5. Complete the hypothesis statement on your Activity Manual page.

6. Read the temperatures on both thermometers.

7. Write them as the beginning temperatures on the chart.

8. Place the thermometers beside each other in a sunny place outside.

9. Wait about an hour. Read the temperatures.

10. Write the ending temperatures for both thermometers in the chart.

11. Find the difference between the beginning temperature and the ending temperature for both thermometers.

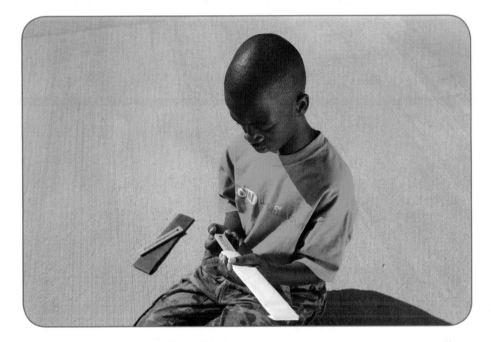

Conclusions

- Did the temperatures stay the same?
- Which thermometer had the greater change in temperature?
- Did the results agree with your hypothesis?
- You learned about colors and temperatures from this test. What can you infer about a car's color and the temperature inside it on a sunny day?

What Living Things Do

What do living things need?

God made you. He made all the things that are around you. He made His creation to praise Him. Some of the things God made are alive. They are living things. **Living** things need food, water, and air to live. They change and grow. All people are living things, including you. Animals are living things. Plants are living things also.

Living and Nonliving Things

Look at the picture and find some living things. Did you see the ducks? Ducks are living things. They need food, water, and air to live. They grow and change. Living things also need space and shelter.

God also made things that are not alive. They are nonliving things. **Nonliving** things do not grow or change. They do not need food, water, and air. God made light. He made air and water. He also made rocks and dirt. These are all nonliving things.

How are living things different from nonliving things?

Basic Needs

Living things have needs. A **need** is what a living thing must have to stay alive.

One of the basic needs of living things is air. You need air to stay alive. You breathe air in and out. Animals breathe air too. Plants do not breathe, but they still need air to stay alive.

Water is another basic need. Some plants and animals need a lot of water. Others need only a small amount. People need plenty of clean water.

The last basic need is food. Food gives energy and helps living things grow. **Energy** is what is needed to cause change. Plants change energy from sunlight to make their own food. Animals and people eat food.

What are three basic needs of living things?

Growing Healthy

You need air, water, and food. These things help you grow and stay healthy. Seeds and plants also need air, water, and food. In this activity you will find out whether bean seeds need soil to grow and be healthy.

Problem

Do bean seeds need soil to grow into healthy plants?

Materials
2 clear plastic cups, 9 oz
paper towels
2 bean seeds
potting soil
water
metric measuring cup
Activity Manual

Procedure

1. Complete the hypothesis in your Activity Manual.
2. Fold the paper towels to fit in one cup.
3. Put a bean seed between the towels and the side of the cup. You should see the seed through the cup.
4. Fill the other cup with potting soil.
5. Plant the other seed in the soil at the edge of the cup. You should see the seed through the cup.
6. Water both cups with 20 milliliters of water.
7. Put both cups in a place where they will get the same amount of light.

8. Observe the cups each day. Watch for any stems or leaves to form. Record your observations in your Activity Manual.

9. Add water as needed to keep the soil and the paper towels wet. Be sure to add the same amount of water to each cup.

Conclusions

- Which young plant was healthier?
- Do bean seeds need soil to help them grow?

Other Needs

Living things need room to live and grow. Small animals can live in small areas. But big animals need larger areas to move. A plant needs space for its roots and branches to grow.

Living things also need shelter. A **shelter** is a safe place to live. Shelters are not the same for all living things. If you live in a house, your house is your shelter. You may have friends or family who live in an apartment. The apartment is their shelter.

Animals need shelter too. They live in many types of shelters. Birds have nests. A fox has a den. A cow may have a barn. An animal's home is its shelter.

Plants do not have homes, but they do need safe places to live. A big tree may protect small plants from getting too much sunlight. It may protect the plants from the wind. The big tree is a shelter for the small plants.

God gave people the job of managing living things. Living things need air, water, and food. They also need space and shelter. Christians should know what living things need. This will help them take care of themselves and other people.

What is a shelter?

Growing and Changing

As living things grow, they change. You have changed. Once you were a baby, but now you are bigger and taller. You are able to do more things by yourself.

The way living things meet their needs may change as they grow. Both a baby and a child need food. A baby needs milk at first. Later the baby eats soft foods. As a baby grows, his teeth grow too. The baby becomes a child like you. A child does not need to eat only soft foods. A child eats other kinds of foods to meet his needs.

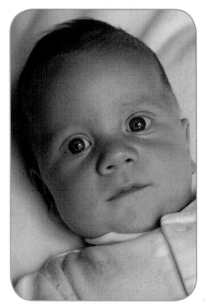

Baby

Toddler

Child

Compare the width of a redwood tree to the width of this log cabin.

Plants also grow and change. Most start out as seeds. Some grow to be tiny flowers, and others grow to be huge trees. Plants and animals grow in different ways. Plants grow new branches and leaves. Hair and fingernails continue to grow on people and animals. But adult animals and people do not make new parts as they grow.

What happens to living things as they grow?

New Living Things

Living things make more living things. God said all living things will make the same kind of living thing. An apple tree will make apples. An apple tree will not make nuts. A fish will have baby fish, not baby snakes.

Plants make more plants. They make seeds, which grow into plants. These young plants look the same as the adult plants.

Animals make new animals. They have babies. A baby animal will be the same kind as its parents. A dog has puppies. A dog does not have kittens.

Animals make baby animals in different ways. Some lay eggs. Other animals make babies inside their bodies. Many babies look like their parents.

Seeds grow into new plants.

Animals make new animals.

A baby cow is called a calf. A baby whale does not look like a cow, but it is also called a calf. Camels and rhinoceroses also have babies that are called calves.

Baby animals grow and change. They become adult animals. Young plants grow. They become adult plants. The adults make new living things. All the stages of the life of a living thing are called a **life cycle**.

What is a life cycle?

A Robin's Life Cycle

A life cycle shows the changes an animal goes through to become an adult. Most animals have a simple life cycle. Their life cycle has three stages: before birth, young, and adult. Most babies look like their parents but are just smaller. The young grow to become adults.

Egg

A mother robin builds a nest from grass and twigs. She lays three to five eggs in the nest. She will sit on her eggs to keep them warm. In about two weeks the eggs will hatch. The egg is the first stage of a robin's life cycle.

Chick

The young are called chicks. The chick is the second stage of a robin's life cycle. The parents feed the chicks fruit and worms. The chicks will grow feathers and learn to fly.

Adult

The chicks will grow and change. As they grow into adults, they can find their own food. The adult is the third stage of a robin's life cycle. An adult will continue the life cycle. It will lay eggs in a nest.

What are the three stages of a robin's life cycle?

A Butterfly's Life Cycle

A butterfly's life cycle has four stages. An adult butterfly lays eggs on a plant. The egg is the first stage. A butterfly does not look like its parents at first.

Caterpillars hatch out of the eggs. This second stage is called a larva. Its main job is to eat and grow. As it gets bigger, it outgrows its skin. It sheds the skin and grows a new one.

At last the caterpillar stops eating. It finds a twig and rests. The caterpillar forms a small sac. The sac keeps the caterpillar safe. This third stage is called a pupa.

Things change inside the sac. The pupa turns into a butterfly with legs and wings. The pupa splits open. An adult butterfly comes out. This is the last stage of the butterfly's life cycle.

The adult butterfly unfolds its wings. It flies away to find food. Soon the butterfly will lay eggs. The life cycle will start again. God designed the caterpillar to change into a beautiful butterfly. Praise God for all the wonderful things He designed!

Butterfly Life Cycle

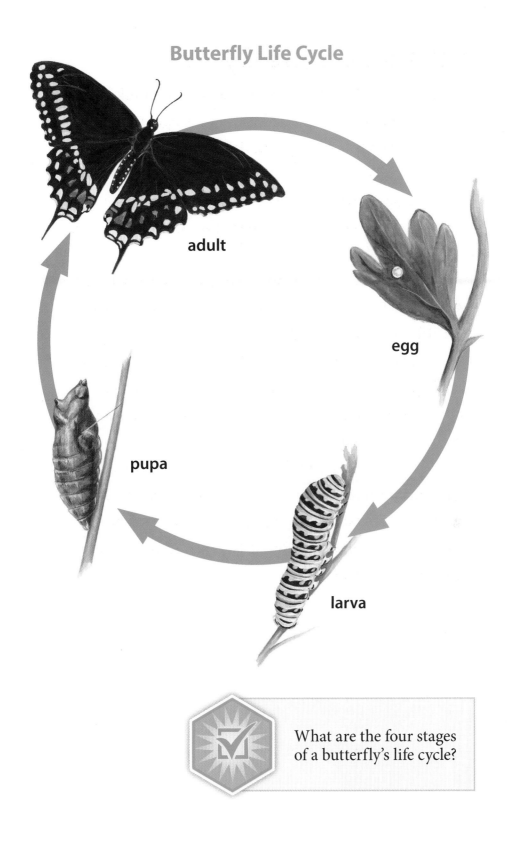

adult

egg

larva

pupa

What are the four stages of a butterfly's life cycle?

3 How Plants Grow

On the third day of Creation, God made plants.
He created different kinds of plants. He made
grasses and flowers. He made trees. He made seeds
for the plants so new plants could grow. The plants
God made give glory to Him.

God also made plants so people could use them. We use plants in many ways. We enjoy flowers. We eat vegetables and fruits. Grasses cover our lawns, and trees give us shade and food. Plants are a good gift from God.

Plant Needs

Plants are living things. They have four basic needs. Plants need water and air. They need soil and light. The soil and light provide the plants' food. Plants need these things to live and grow.

Plants also need space to live and grow. Their roots need room to spread in the soil. Their leaves need room to gather sunlight. Plants that are too close together may not get what they need to live and grow.

Plants live in hot places and cold places. They live in sunlight and shade. Some plants need a lot of water. Other plants can live with very little water. Plants can live in soil and on rocks. They live in places that supply their needs.

What are four basic needs of plants?

Plant Parts

God made most plants with four parts to help them get what they need. Each part of a plant has a job.

Leaves

Leaves make food for the plant. They take in sunlight and air. The leaves use sunlight, air, water, and **nutrients** from the soil to make food. Nutrients are the things found in food that are needed for life and growth.

Roots

Roots take in water and nutrients from the soil. They help hold the plant in the ground.

Flowers

Many plants also have flowers. The **flowers** make seeds.

Stems

The **stems** hold the plant upright. They hold up the leaves and the flowers. Stems move water and nutrients from the roots to the leaves. Stems move food from the leaves to other parts of the plant.

What are the parts of a plant?

A Plant's Life Cycle

When God created plants, He said each would make the same kind of plant. This means a bean seed will grow to be a bean plant.

Parts of a Seed

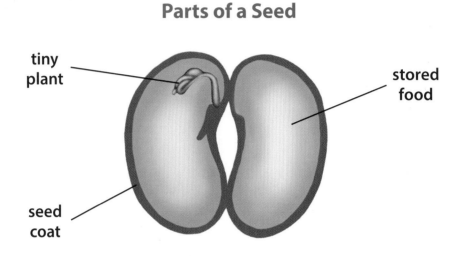

tiny plant

stored food

seed coat

The stages of a plant's life are called its life cycle. Most new plants grow from seeds. Seeds have different parts. The covering on the outside is called the seed coat. Inside the seed is stored food and a tiny plant.

When a seed drops, the tiny plant inside may start to grow. It uses the nutrients in the stored food. The seed also needs the right amount of water and warmth to sprout.

Soon the seed coat breaks open, and a tiny root comes out. The root grows down. Then a stem grows up, and the plant's leaves open. This young plant is called a **seedling**.

The seedling keeps growing. More leaves and stems grow. The seedling becomes an adult plant. The adult plant makes flowers, and the flowers make new seeds. The life cycle continues as the seeds start to grow.

Plant Life Cycle

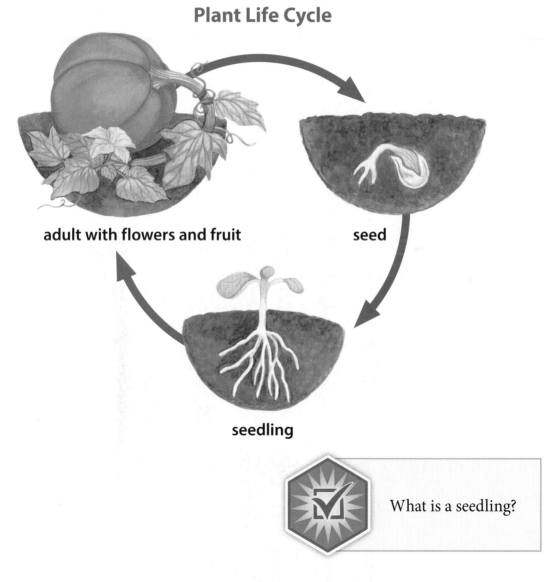

adult with flowers and fruit

seed

seedling

What is a seedling?

EXPLORATION

Plants We Eat

One of the main reasons God created plants was for us to eat them. To be healthy you should eat fruits and vegetables every day. Some might be roots, and others may be stems or leaves. What part of a plant is your favorite to eat?

What to Do

1. Collect pictures, labels, and packages from vegetables and fruits that you eat.

2. Sort them into groups of roots, stems, leaves, flowers, fruit, or seeds.

3. Make a poster to display your groups.

4. Show your poster to others and tell what you have learned.

Seeds

Most new plants grow from seeds. Seeds are found in many shapes, sizes, and colors. The seeds of many adult plants grow in the flowers. One sunflower can have hundreds of seeds. Grains are types of grass that give us seeds to eat. Corn is a kind of grain.

Some flowers grow into fruit. The seeds are hidden inside the fruit. The fruit covers and protects the seeds. Fruits can grow on trees, bushes, and vines. Apples and pumpkins are fruits with seeds inside.

Sunflower seeds

Corn seeds

Pumpkin seeds

What is grain?

How Seeds Travel

Think about what plants need to live and grow. Their roots need room to get food and water. What would happen if all an adult plant's seeds fell around it? The roots of the adult and the new plants may not get enough food and water.

Many seeds are able to travel away from the plant before they start to grow. There are many ways seeds are scattered, or spread.

Wind may blow seeds from one place to another. Some seeds are shaped to fly in the wind. Seeds may also fall into water and float away to a new place.

• Meet the Scientist • George de Mestral

George de Mestral was an inventor. One day he went for a walk with his dog. He noticed that seeds stuck to his dog's fur. He then studied the seeds. He saw that they had tiny hooks that grabbed the fur. This gave him the idea for a fastener for clothes. He named his invention Velcro.

Animals may carry seeds to new places. Some animals pick up a fruit to eat it. The seeds in the fruit are dropped in a new place. Some seeds stick to animals' fur. These seeds may take a ride before being dropped in a new place.

 What are some ways seeds are scattered?

Traveling Seeds

Many seeds sprout away from their adult plants. Different seeds are scattered in different ways. You will be testing seeds to see how they can travel.

Problem

How are seeds scattered?

Materials
seed mixture
white paper
tape
fuzzy stuffed animal
container of water
hand lens
Activity Manual

Procedure

1. Spread your seeds on the paper. Choose 2 different kinds of seeds to test. Keep 5 of each that you chose and return the other seeds to the container.

2. Tape 1 of each kind of seed to the Hypothesis chart on the Activity Manual page.

3. Circle the ways that you think each seed is scattered.

4. Test each type of seed to see whether either can be moved by wind. Place 1 of each type of seed in the space on your Activity Manual page. Gently blow on the seeds.

5. Observe if they move. Tape each seed where it lands.

6. Test each type of seed to see whether either can be carried. Place 1 of each seed on the fuzzy stuffed animal. Pick up the stuffed animal and gently shake it.

7. Observe whether either seed sticks to the stuffed animal. Tape each seed to match your observations.

8. Test each type of seed to see whether either can float in water. Place 1 of each seed in the container of water.

9. Observe whether either seed floats. Tape each seed to match your observations.

10. Classify your seeds by the way they traveled.

11. Compare your results with your hypothesis.

Conclusions

- Do your results agree with your hypothesis?
- Describe something about how each seed looks that might cause it to be scattered in the way that you observed.

4

Where Things Live

God created all living things. They live in many different places. They live near other living things that are like them. They have different jobs to do.

God created people in His own image. He gave them the job of caring for the plants and animals. We should learn about the places plants and animals live in order to care for them. Learning about these places helps you honor God in your work.

Populations and Communities

All the living things of one kind in one area are called a **population**. All the deer in one area make up the deer population. A turtle is not part of the deer population. It is part of the turtle population.

Populations can be different sizes. The deer population can be large if many deer live in one area. The same area may have only a few turtles. The turtle population is smaller.

All the different populations make up a community. A **community** is all the living things in one area. People live in communities. They have different jobs to do. They live in different homes. The people in a community depend on each other.

Animals and plants live in communities too. There are the plants and animals you can see. There are also small living things that you cannot see.

All the living things in a community work together. Plants make food for the animals. They also provide shelter for animals. Animals can be food for each other. All the living things depend on each other.

How is a population different from a community?

Environments

God made all nonliving things. An **environment** is all the nonliving things that are around a living thing. Water, air, and soil are nonliving things. Weather and sunlight are also nonliving things. The environment is very important. It meets the needs of the living things that live there.

Different animals may need different environments. You would not find a polar bear in a desert. You would also not see a cactus in a snowy place. The polar bear and the cactus need different environments.

Habitats

God gave every living thing a place to live. A **habitat** is a place to live. It is a place where a living thing can find food, water, and shelter. Habitats are part of larger areas. They are part of an environment.

Habitats can be in many places. They can be in water. They can be in a tree. They can be underground. Many different habitats can provide for the needs of plants and animals.

What is an environment?

57

There are many kinds of habitats on the earth. Some places have cold weather. Others have hot weather. Some places are wet, and others are dry. In each place there are plants and animals. God made the living things in each place to fit their habitat.

The Desert

The desert habitat is a hot and dry place. It gets very little rain. The plants and animals there do not need a lot of water. Most plants are able to store water. Most animals get the water they need from the food they eat.

Cactus

Desert tortoise

One of the plants that grows in the desert is the cactus. It soaks up water and stores it to use later. Another desert plant is the sage. It grows in warm weather and dry soil. It has white or purple flowers.

The desert tortoise holds water under its shell. It digs tunnels to stay in when it is hot. Lizards and snakes also dig under the ground to stay cool.

There are many deserts around the world. The Sahara in Africa is the largest. It is almost as large as the United States.

Creation Corner

Camels are desert animals. People used to think camels stored water in their humps. Now we know that the humps store fat. God made them so they could go a long time without food and water. They can go for two weeks without drinking water at all! When they do drink water, they drink a lot at one time.

What kind of habitat is the desert?

The Rain Forest

The rain forest is a hot and wet habitat. It rains almost every day in this habitat. Many animals and plants live here.

There are many tall trees in the rain forest. They supply food and shelter for animals. Monkeys live in and around the trees. They eat the fruits and nuts in the trees.

The largest rain forest is in South America. It is along the Amazon River.

Monkey

The Tundra

The tundra is a cold and dry habitat. It is covered with snow most of the year. Because of the cold, only a few kinds of plants can grow. Grass and small plants grow there. But the growing season is too short for trees.

Many animals that live in the tundra have thick fur to keep warm. Some animals have fur that changes color. The Arctic fox and the Arctic hare have white fur in the winter. This makes it easier for them to hide in the snow. In spring their fur changes to brown. This helps them hide from other animals when the snow melts.

Arctic fox

 What are the differences between a rain forest and a tundra?

61

The Woodland Forest

The woodland forest habitat has many trees and bushes. The weather changes with the seasons. The forest is warm in the summer. But it is cold in the winter.

The forest community works together. Trees and bushes provide shelter. Birds build nests in the trees. Some raccoons have homes in the tree roots. Deer hide among the bushes and ferns.

The forest gets enough rain for plants to grow well. Plants provide food for animals. Berries and seeds grow in the trees and bushes. Many animals eat them.

Raccoon

Animals help the forest as well. Squirrels bury seeds. Some of the seeds grow into new plants. Woodpeckers help the trees by eating harmful bugs.

In the winter some trees lose their leaves. Sometimes animals cannot find what they need to live. Some go to warmer places. Some go into their homes and sleep all winter.

Woodpecker

Why do some forest animals move away or sleep during the winter?

The Ocean

Some plants and animals make their homes in water habitats. But not all water habitats are the same. Some are in salt water. Some are in fresh water.

The ocean is a saltwater habitat. Plants such as seaweed and seagrass live near the surface of the ocean. They need sunlight to make food. Many animals also live here. Some eat the plants. Or they eat the animals that eat the plants. Dolphins live near the ocean's surface. They eat fish and squid.

Dolphin

Fantastic Facts

Not all forests are on land. Kelp forests are thick clumps of seaweed growing close together. Some kinds of kelp can grow more than 100 feet tall. Many fish and other animals live in kelp forests.

Some plants and animals live in coral reefs. Coral reefs need sunlight to make food. So they live in shallow, warm places in the ocean. The shallow waters are as much as 200 feet deep. Many colorful fish live in these reefs.

Plants and animals also live deep in the ocean. There it is cold and dark. Some animals that live there make their own light, such as hatchet fish.

Coral reef

A hatchet fish

What kind of habitat is the ocean?

The Pond

Freshwater habitats include rivers, lakes, and ponds. A pond is smaller than a lake. Some pond habitats are in or on the water. Other habitats are on the land along the pond edges.

Fish live in the pond. Plants give the fish places to hide from birds and other animals. Cattails and water lilies are water plants. They live at the surface of the water. Insects fly here and there among the plants. Frogs and turtles use the plants for shelter.

Dragonfly

Ducks, otters, and muskrats live along the banks. Ducks build nests in the grass and bushes. The ducks' webbed feet help them swim. They eat the plants and fish in the pond. Otters and muskrats may make burrows, or holes, in the pond banks. Otters feed on fish and frogs while muskrats eat mostly plants.

Duck

What do ducks have that help them swim?

Home Sweet Home

A zoo is full of animals. They are brought from habitats around the world. Their habitats were places they could find food, water, and shelter. Some zoo habitats have one animal. Other habitats have many. A zookeeper plans each new habitat to meet the needs of the animals that will live there.

In this activity you will make a model, or an example, of a new habitat for a zoo.

Purpose

Model a habitat.

Materials
resources about
  habitats
shoebox
craft supplies
Activity Manual

Procedure

1. Choose which habitat you want to model in the shoebox. Record your choice in your Activity Manual.

2. Use resources to find out about the habitat. Record the information.

3. Plan what living and nonliving things you will include in your model habitat. You must have at least one kind of plant and two kinds of animals.

4. Think about the materials you will use to represent the living and nonliving things. You may use rocks, plants, and toy animals. You may draw or find pictures.

5. Sketch your plans in your Activity Manual.

6. Cut out the card from the Activity Manual. Attach it to your shoebox.

7. Present your model and share what you have learned about the habitat.

Conclusions

• How do your living things survive in their habitat?

• Where would that kind of habitat actually be found on the earth? Explain why this habitat could or could not meet your needs if you lived there.

5

What Fossils Show Us

Scientists can study things they observe. But how do they find out about things they cannot observe? Scientists cannot observe the earth's past. They must use clues to try to find out what happened. One way to find out is to dig in the ground and study rocks. Rocks give clues about the earth's past.

Creation or Evolution?

Scientists use what they believe to explain the clues they find. Their beliefs are their worldview. A **worldview** is a way of looking at or understanding the world.

There are two main beliefs about how the earth was made. One is called Creation. The other is called evolution.

The Bible says that God spoke and made the earth. People who believe in **Creation** believe this. They believe that God created all things. They believe that what the Bible says is true. They have a biblical worldview.

God made the earth perfect. But when Adam sinned, God cursed the earth. It was changed from being a perfect place. It became a place with sin and death in it.

The sin of people caused God to send a flood. The Flood covered the whole earth. People, animals, and plants on the earth died. The earth was very different after the Flood.

Other people believe in **evolution.** They think that the earth came about by chance. They believe that it changed many times. They believe that the changes were made slowly over a long time. Their worldview is not based on the Bible.

Scientists share the clues they find. But they explain the clues in different ways. Some scientists have a biblical worldview. Other scientists do not. What they believe affects how they understand what they see.

Grand Canyon

How does someone who believes in Creation think the world began?

Following Clues

EXPLORATION

Scientists study clues to find out about the earth. They study clues to find out about the things that lived long ago. You can study clues like a scientist.

What to do

1. Look at the trail of footprints your teacher made. Imagine you are a scientist who discovered this trail.

2. Look for clues. Answer the questions in your Activity Manual.

3. Write and draw what you can infer about the animal that made the footprints.

4. Compare your findings with those of others.

Fossils

Scientists use rocks to find out about the earth's past. Many important clues come from fossils that are found in rocks. Other kinds of fossils also give clues.

A **fossil** is the remains of a living thing that died long ago. Fossils form when living things are buried quickly by mud or sand.

People think differently about fossils. Some think fossils formed over millions of years. These people believe in evolution. Others think most fossils formed during the Flood. These people believe in Creation.

The Flood moved a lot of mud. The mud quickly buried some living things. After the Flood, the mud dried. Fossils formed as the mud dried. Fossils are found all over the earth. They are found in deserts and prairies. They are even found on mountains.

What is a fossil?

Kinds of Fossils

Fossils form in different ways. In some fossils the living thing dies and turns to rock. These are called petrified fossils.

Petrified wood

Sometimes mud hardens around a living thing. The living thing dies and rots. It leaves its shape in the rock. This kind of fossil is called a mold.

A mold sometimes fills with mud. The hardened mud becomes rock. This kind of fossil is called a cast. The cast is a copy of the living thing that was once in the mold.

Cast

Mold

Amber is a fossil that is not rock. It is tree sap that hardened. Amber can contain other fossils. Sometimes insects were trapped by the sticky sap. They are still seen in the hardened amber.

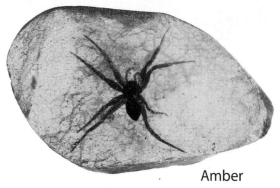

Amber

Scientists have found fossils in places where the land is always frozen. They are called frozen fossils. Most frozen fossils are large animals. One kind of frozen fossil is of the woolly mammoth. Woolly mammoths look like hairy elephants. The fossils of these mammoths show they were buried quickly and then frozen. Some still had food in their stomachs and seeds in their mouths!

Woolly mammoth

List five kinds of fossils.

Dinosaur Fossils

Many fossils show animals that are no longer alive. Some of these fossils are of dinosaurs. Dinosaurs lived long ago. But now dinosaurs are extinct. **Extinct** means that none of the animals of that kind are still alive.

Tyrannosaurus rex fossil

We know that dinosaurs were once alive. The Bible describes some animals that may have been dinosaurs. Scientists have found dinosaur fossils. Some fossils that have been found are dinosaur eggs. That is how scientists know that some dinosaurs laid eggs.

You may think of dinosaurs as very large animals. We know from their bones that some dinosaurs were very large. But not all dinosaurs were big. They were many different sizes. Some were as small as chickens.

What does it mean when we say that dinosaurs are extinct?

Sometimes most of a dinosaur's bones are found in one place. Scientists try to fit the bones together. Fitting the bones together is like a big puzzle.

Sometimes scientists find only a few bones. They have to guess what the skeleton looked like. They must guess which bones are missing. And they must guess what those missing bones looked like.

Even with a whole skeleton, scientists do not know much about what the living dinosaur looked like. They do not know what kind of skin it had or what color it was. They do not know for certain what it ate or what kind of weather was best for it.

Dinosaur bones are fossils found in rock.

Dinosaurs

There are many kinds of dinosaur fossils. This tells us that there were many kinds of dinosaurs. You might think that all dinosaurs were mean and scary. But dinosaurs were much like animals today. Some ate plants, and some ate meat.

The *Stegosaurus* was about the size of a bus. An adult was 6–10 meters (20–30 feet) long.

Science and the Bible

Some people believe that dinosaurs lived millions of years before humans. They call that time "prehistory." But there is no prehistory. The Bible is our written history. It tells of the world from the time of Creation. God created the dinosaurs at the same time He created animals.

It weighed more than 3100 kilograms (3 tons). It had two rows of bony plates along its back. On its tail it had four long spikes. The *Stegosaurus* may have used its tail to defend itself from other dinosaurs. Although the *Stegosaurus* may have looked scary, it ate only plants.

What is one thing that a skeleton cannot tell you about a dinosaur?

The *Tyrannosaurus rex* was a large dinosaur that probably ate meat. It was about 13 meters (40 feet) long. And it weighed about twice as much as the *Stegosaurus*. The head of the *Tyrannosaurus rex* was over a meter (3 feet) long and had sharp, strong teeth.

The *Tyrannosaurus rex* stood on its back legs. It had very short front legs. Scientists are not sure how the short legs helped the dinosaur. The legs were too short for walking or for reaching the dinosaur's mouth.

A *Tyrannosaurus rex* tooth could be 15 cm (6 inches) long.

The End of Dinosaurs

Most people and land animals died during the Flood. Before the Flood, God told a man named Noah to build an ark. The ark was to keep Noah and his family safe. God also told Noah to take animals on the ark. Noah took two of every kind of animal including dinosaurs.

After the Flood, the earth changed. Dinosaurs may not have been able to meet their needs. They became extinct. Today what we know about dinosaurs comes from the clues fossils give us.

Name one possible reason that dinosaurs became extinct.

83

Bag of Bones

When scientists find dinosaur bones, they seldom find the bones together. They must try to figure out how the bones fit to form a skeleton.

In this activity you will use a bag of loose "bones" to build a model of a dinosaur skeleton.

Purpose

Make a model of a dinosaur skeleton.

> **Materials**
> bag of "bones"
> large sheet of
>   construction paper
> glue
> crayons or markers
> Activity Manual

Procedure

1. Spread your "bones" on your paper.

2. Arrange your bones to form a skeleton. Design the skeleton with features you want.

3. Draw an outline of the dinosaur around the skeleton. Add any additional features, such as horns or spikes.

4. Label the ribs, leg bones, backbone, skull, and other parts of the skeleton.

5. Give your dinosaur a name. Write it above your skeleton and on your Activity Manual page.

6. Write a paragraph describing your dinosaur. Include details about its size, where it lived, and what it ate.

Conclusions

- Could you have made a different dinosaur using the same bag of bones?
- What would you need in order to know what a dinosaur looked like?

6 What Makes Up the Earth

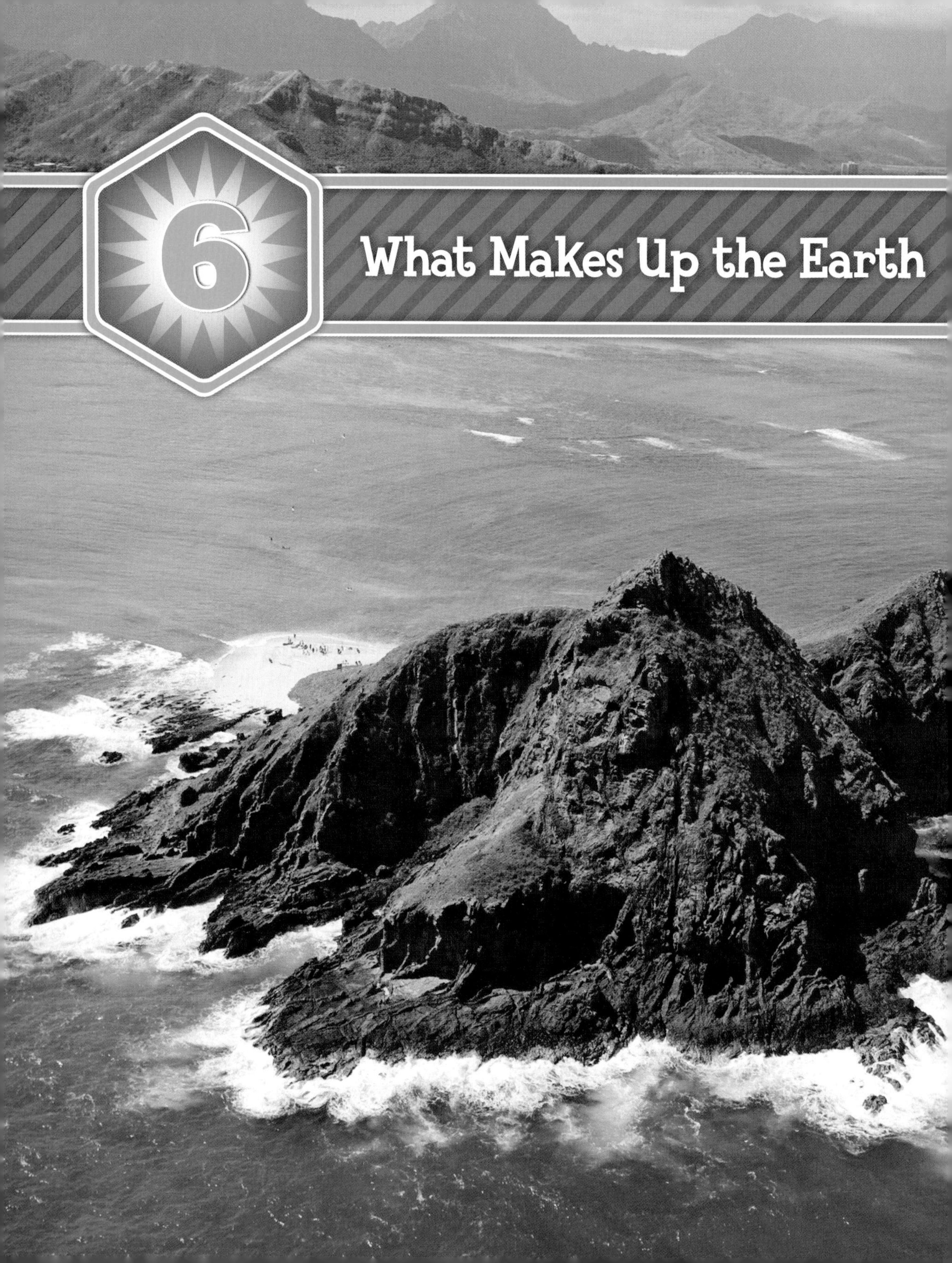

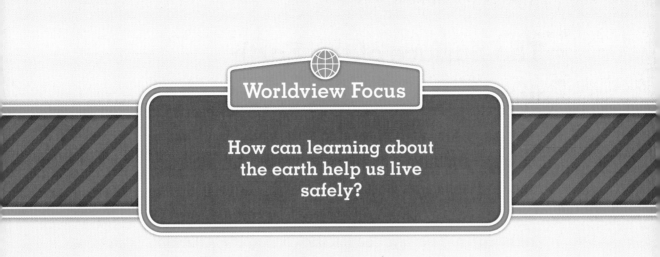

You have been learning that each living thing needs a place to live. Living things live in places all over the earth. On the first day of Creation, God created the earth. He covered it with water. Then God caused dry land to appear. He made the earth with both land and seas. Sadly, because of sin, sometimes the earth is dangerous. Learning about the land and the sea can help us live safely and keep others safe.

The Surface of the Earth

Water

Most of the earth is covered with water. Look at the graph and map. You can see that about three-fourths of the earth is water. The large bodies of salt water are called oceans. There are four main oceans on the earth. They are the Pacific Ocean, the Atlantic Ocean, the Indian Ocean, and the Arctic Ocean. Some of the smaller bodies of salt water are called seas and gulfs.

Many living things find their home in salt water. Whales, shrimp, and seaweed are some of the things that live in salt water.

Fresh water is found in rain and on land. Bodies of fresh water include lakes, ponds, rivers, and streams. People depend on sources of clean fresh water to drink. Plants and animals living on land also need clean fresh water.

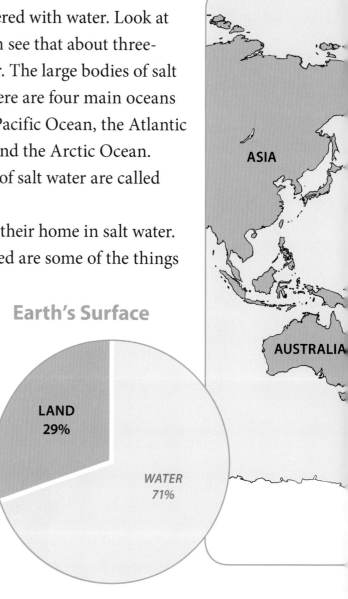

Earth's Surface

LAND
29%

WATER
71%

ASIA

AUSTRALIA

Oceans and Continents

How much of the earth is covered with water?

Land

Water is not the only thing that covers the earth's surface. There is also land. The large areas of land are called continents. There are seven continents. They are Africa, Antarctica, Asia, Australia, Europe, North America, and South America.

Some of the continents are connected. Others are not. Australia is an island— an area of land completely surrounded by water. Antarctica is not connected to other areas of land either. It is covered with ice and snow.

All of the land does not look the same. Some landforms you might see are mountains, canyons, and plains. Some places are covered with grass or trees. Other places are mostly rock or sand. Each place is home to animals and plants and often people.

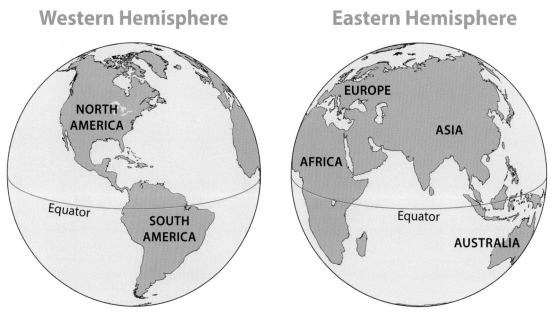

The earth can be divided into halves called hemispheres.

Mountains, valley, and lake in the Alps of Switzerland

Tiger Leaping Gorge along the Yangtze River in China

What are the large areas of land on the earth's surface called?

Serengeti Plain in Tanzania, Africa

The Inside of the Earth

We can find out about the surface of the earth. We live on it. We can observe and measure it. But the earth is more than what we see on the surface. Most of the earth is under the surface.

It is not as easy to find out about the inside of the earth. Scientists cannot open the earth and look inside. They use what happens on the surface to understand and infer what happens inside.

Giant Crystal Cave in Mexico

Studying the Inside of the Earth

Scientists study caves and other openings in the earth's surface. They may dig large holes. They study rocks and how they form.

Some scientists drill holes in the earth's surface. They pull out samples of rock. They study the rock and record things about it. They record what materials are in the rock. They record what layers of rock are in the sample and how deep the sample was.

Scientists dig and drill to study layers of rock. They sometimes work with other people who dig and drill. People dig to find coal, gold, and other minerals. People drill to find water or oil. Scientists can help them work safely.

Drilling for oil

What are two ways that scientists can study the inside of the earth?

The Layers of the Earth

Scientists think the earth is made of three main layers. The outside layer is mostly solid rock. It is called the **crust**. The part of the earth we see is the surface of the crust.

The earth's crust is a thin layer. If the earth were an apple, the crust would be as thin as the apple's peel. The crust is thinner under the oceans. It is about 5 kilometers (3 miles) at the thinnest place. Continents are thicker. The thickest part of the crust is about 70 kilometers (30 miles). It may seem that scientists drill very deep holes. But they have not been able to drill past the crust.

Under the crust is a layer called the **mantle**. The mantle is much thicker than the crust. Scientists think the mantle is about 2900 kilometers (1,800 miles) thick. If the earth were the size of an apple, the mantle would be the white part of the apple.

The mantle is very hot. It is made of hot, melted rock. This melted rock is what comes from some volcanoes.

Deep in the earth is the third layer. Like the center of an apple, the center of the earth is called the **core**. The core is about 7100 kilometers (4,400 miles) across.

The core has two parts. It has an outer core that is liquid. Scientists believe that the very center, or the inner core, is solid iron. The core is hotter than the mantle. It is the hottest part of the earth.

Layers of the Earth

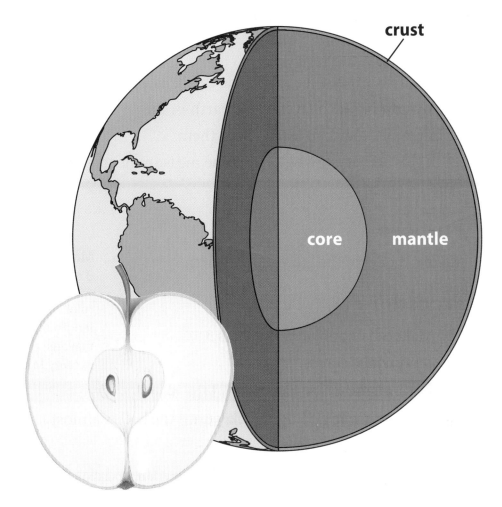

crust

core   mantle

What are the three main layers of the earth?

The Earth's Layers

Scientists cannot see inside the earth. They cannot know exactly how big each layer of the earth is. But by using certain tools, they can learn about them.

In this activity you will use some measurements to make a model of the earth's layers.

Purpose

Make a model of the layers of the earth.

Procedure

1. Make a ball of blue clay that is 3 centimeters across.

2. Press a layer of red clay around the blue ball. Continue adding red clay until the ball is almost 6 centimeters across.

3. Use the green clay to completely cover the red clay ball with a thin layer.

4. Hold the thread tightly between both hands. Slice through the middle of the clay ball with the thread.

5. Draw a picture of the inside of your model in your Activity Manual. Color the picture to show the layers.

6. Label the layers of the earth that your model shows.

Materials
3 colors of clay (red, blue, and green)
ruler
length of thread
crayons
Activity Manual

Conclusions

- Infer which layer of the earth is the thinnest.
- Infer which layer of the earth is in the center.

The Moving Surface

The surface of the earth does not stay the same. Parts of it move at different times. Scientists study these movements. What they learn helps them understand the parts under the surface.

Volcanoes

A **volcano** is an opening in the earth's surface. This opening allows hot, melted rock to flow out. This melted rock comes from deep within the mantle. The melted rock that comes out of a volcano is called **lava**. A volcano may slowly ooze lava out of the earth. But sometimes a volcano erupts. When this happens, hot lava sprays up into the air.

When a volcano erupts, it often changes the earth's surface. Its power may blow the top off a mountain. A volcano can also build up land. As the lava hardens, it makes new land. Volcanoes can form mountains. A volcano under the ocean can form an island. The Hawaiian Islands were made by volcanoes.

 What is the melted rock that comes from a volcano called?

Mount St. Helens

Earthquakes

Scientists also find out about the inside of the earth through earthquakes. An **earthquake** happens when large areas of the earth's surface shake and move. The earthquake causes parts of the earth to move back and forth. Scientists measure how long the earth shakes. They also measure how much the earth moves.

Collapsed road after an earthquake

Scientists use a machine called a seismograph. This machine records the earth's movements. The scientists can tell things about the inside of the earth by how the earth moves.

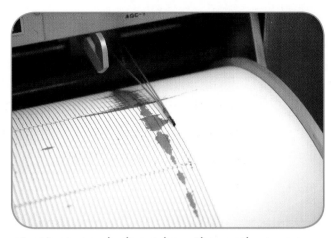

A seismograph shows how the earth moves during an earthquake.

Earthquakes and volcanoes are related to each other. Earthquakes may create openings in the earth's surface where melted rock can flow out. A volcano may erupt and cause the earth's surface to move suddenly. This can cause an earthquake.

Earthquakes under the ocean can cause large waves to form. These waves, called tsunamis, can destroy buildings and harm people.

Volcanoes and earthquakes can be dangerous. Scientists study what happens on the surface of the earth. What they find out can help them infer about the inside of the earth. They can use what they learn to keep people safe.

What does a seismograph do?

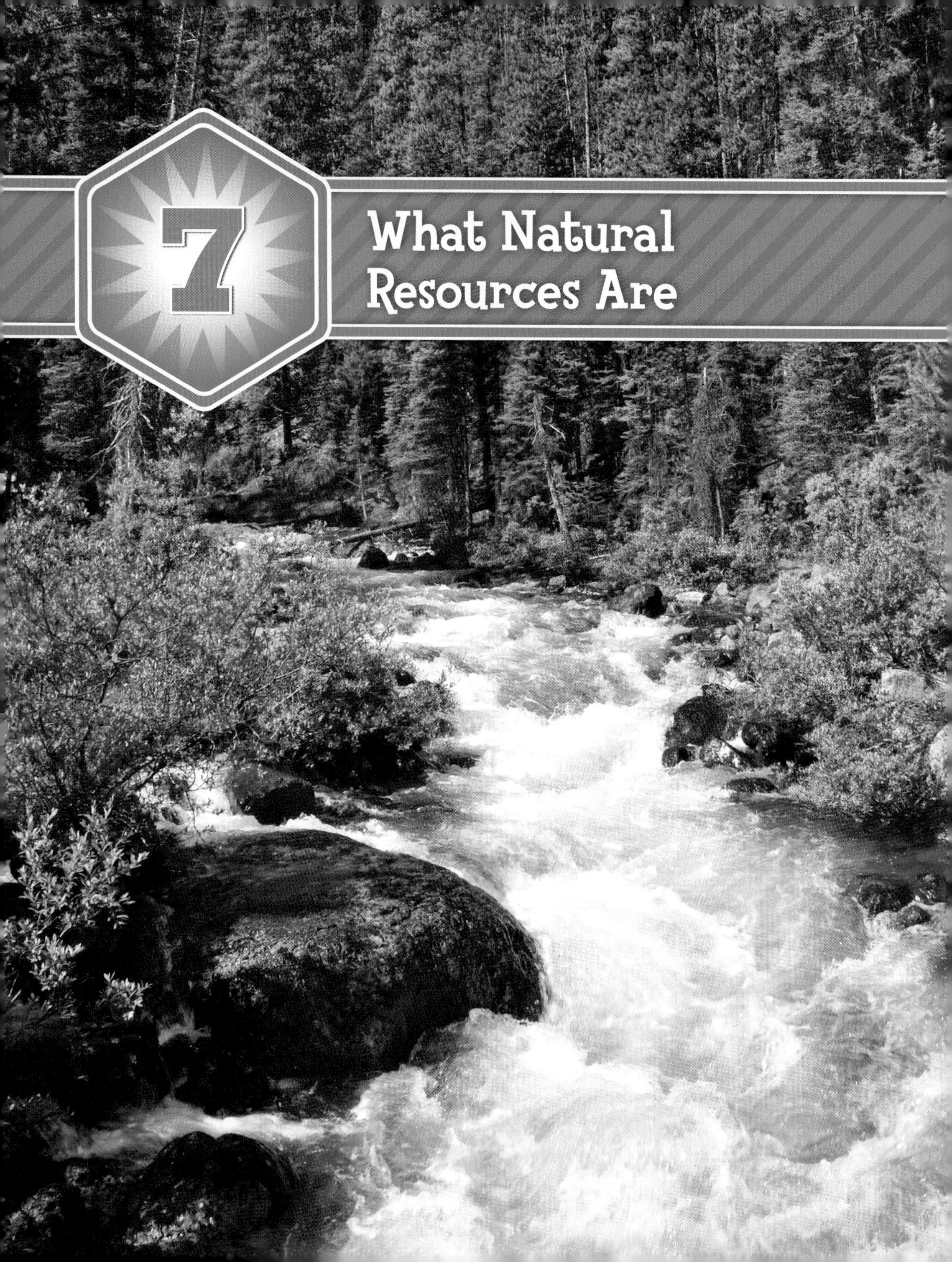

7 What Natural Resources Are

**How can we conserve the
earth's natural resources?**

God created the earth for His glory. He provided fresh water for plants to grow. He gave us gas to heat our homes and cook our meals. He provided everything we need to live on the earth.

Every living thing uses resources to supply its basic needs. A **natural resource** is a material in nature that God made for people's use. Our food, water, and shelter come from natural resources. God wants us to take care of these resources and not waste them. Taking care of God's world honors Him. It is a way to obey God's command to love your neighbor.

103

Natural Resources

Our natural resources include water, soil, trees, and fossil fuels. We need to use them to meet our needs. It is not easy to use natural resources without harming nature. So we need to study the earth to find better and safer ways to use resources. We should conserve the earth's natural resources. To **conserve** means to not waste. It means to use something wisely.

Water

Water is one of our natural resources. We drink it. We play in it. We use it to water plants that provide food for us. Water is one of the basic needs of living things.

Remember that most of the earth is covered by water. With so much water, it seems there would be plenty for living things. But most water on the earth is salty. And most living things must have fresh water.

• Meet the Scientist •   Jacques-Yves Cousteau

An oceanographer is a scientist who studies the ocean. Jacques-Yves Cousteau was a famous French oceanographer. He is best known for helping invent the scuba. A scuba is an air tank that allows you to breathe under water. Divers have used this gear to explore the ocean in ways that they could not before. Cousteau also made several underwater films. His television films brought the wonders of the ocean to everyone.

God sends rain and snow to the earth. This helps give us fresh water. But we should also take care of the fresh water on the earth. We need to keep it clean so it can be used for drinking and bathing.

We should also conserve water. There are many ways you and your family can help. Turn off the water when you are not using it. Wash clothes or dishes only when you have a full load.

Plants need water to grow.

What is a natural resource?

Soil

On the surface of the earth is a layer of soil. Soil is a natural resource. Without soil, most plants will not grow. Plants provide food for people and animals. God gave us soil so we can grow food.

Sometimes soil on the earth's surface is moved from one place to another. We call this **erosion**. Wind and water can cause erosion. Erosion can remove soil needed for plants.

We try to keep soil from eroding. Farmers plow fields in certain ways to prevent erosion. We plant trees and other plants to help hold soil in place. The plants' roots help prevent erosion.

A field plowed to help prevent erosion

Trees

Trees are another natural resource. We get fruit and nuts from trees.

We use wood from trees for many things. Most houses have a frame that is made of wood. Many kinds of furniture are also made from wood. Even your notebook paper is made from wood.

Trees can be replaced. But we still need to use them wisely. Trees take years to grow. We must be careful not to cut them down faster than newly planted trees can grow.

What is erosion?

Fossil Fuels

During the Flood some living things formed fossils. But most living things died and were crushed. Their remains formed fossil fuels.

Fossil fuels are natural resources formed when plants and animals are buried quickly. Oil, coal, and natural gas are fossil fuels. Some resources can be replaced or put back. But we cannot replace fossil fuels.

We use fossil fuels to produce energy. Most electricity is made by burning fossil fuels. We also use fossil fuels for heating. We make gasoline from oil. Gasoline powers many cars, trucks, and other machines.

Fossil fuels provide a good source of power. But they also cause pollution. **Pollution** is anything that makes the air, water, or land dirty. Spilled oil can destroy plants and animals. When we burn fossil fuels, we can cause air pollution. You can see the air pollution sometimes in cities where there are many cars.

Polluted air over a city

God gave us fossil fuels to use. But people should use them wisely. You can help conserve these resources. Turn off the lights when you leave a room. Turn off the electronic game when you are done playing. Doing these things can conserve fossil fuels.

What are fossil fuels?

The Three Rs

There are many things that you can do to help conserve the resources God gave us. A good way to conserve is to remember the three Rs. The three Rs stand for *reuse*, *reduce*, and *recycle*.

Reuse

When we **reuse**, we use something again. Maybe the old towels at your house have become rags for cleaning. The towels are being reused. The plastic bags from the grocery store may become trash bags. The plastic bags are being reused in bathroom trash cans.

Reusing a shirt

You can find many ways to reuse things. You can cover an old can and use it to hold pencils. You may use an old shirt from your dad or big brother for an art shirt. Maybe something was delivered to your house in a box. That box can be reused to pack away other things.

Reduce

When we **reduce**, we use less of something. Many companies try to reduce. Some are using less paper. Most grocery store bags are used once and thrown away. Stores now offer bags that can be reused. This reduces the amount of plastic bags thrown away. Some items are sold in smaller packages. The smaller packages use less cardboard and plastic.

There are many ways you can reduce. Turn off the water while you are brushing your teeth. Close outside doors when the heat or air conditioning is on. Turn off the lights when you leave a room. Use a lunch box instead of a paper bag. Draw on both sides of a sheet of paper.

Reducing water use helps conserve this natural resource.

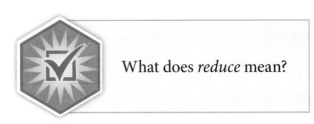

What does *reduce* mean?

Recycle

To make something new out of an object is to **recycle**. Sometimes the new object is the same kind of thing as the old one. You can buy recycled note cards. They are made from paper that has been recycled. Some plastic bottles are made from recycled plastic bottles. Tires may be cut up and used on playgrounds.

Often the new object is not the same as the old object. Plastic bottles can become picnic tables or park benches. Aluminum cans may become picture frames or key chains.

Perhaps you use a box at home for recycling. This box is called a recycling bin. Items are put into the bin. Then the bin is placed on your street next to the trash can. Workers in a recycling truck pick up the items.

Recycling center

You may need to go to a recycling center in order to recycle. This center has many bins. Your things must be sorted and put into the correct bins. Then the items can be recycled.

There are many items you can recycle. Newspaper and cardboard can be recycled. You can also recycle aluminum, glass, plastic, and rubber.

God gave us many natural resources to use. The three Rs help us use these resources wisely. Even through small tasks, you can help conserve our resources.

Recycling old newspapers

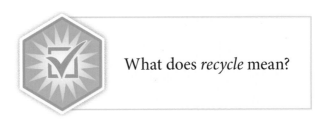

What does *recycle* mean?

Recycled Paper

We need to conserve the earth's natural resources. Trees are one of our natural resources. Different kinds of paper are made from trees. Newspaper is made from trees. When newspaper is recycled, new paper can be made. In this activity you will recycle old newspapers to make new paper.

Purpose

Recycle newspapers to make new paper.

Materials
newspaper
water
metric measuring
  cups
potato masher
large dishpan
wire screen
dishtowel
Activity Manual

Procedure

1. Tear several sheets of newspaper into small pieces.
2. Pour 600 milliliters of water into a bowl. Add the pieces of newspaper. Make sure each piece gets wet.
3. Mash and stir the paper with the potato masher for several minutes.
4. Pour 3000 milliliters of water into the dishpan. Add the mashed newspaper. Use the masher to spread it evenly through the water.
5. Press the wire screen to the bottom of the pan. Gently move the screen back and forth.

6. Slowly lift the screen out of the pan. Hold the screen over the pan for about 1 minute to let the extra water drain off.

7. Set the screen on top of some extra newspaper. Cover with a towel. Press down on the towel to squeeze more water from the screen and pulp.

8. Remove the towel. Gently peel off your new paper. Set it aside to dry.

Conclusions

- How is the new paper different from the old newspaper?

- What could you use this new paper for?

- How does recycling newspaper and other things help Christians obey God's command to love your neighbor?

8

How the Earth Moves

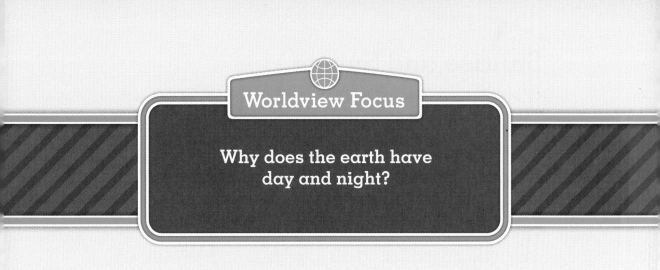

When God first created the earth, everything was dark. There was no sun or stars or moon. Then God said, "Let there be light." God gave the name *day* to the light and *night* to the darkness. Later He created the sun to shine in the day. He created the stars and moon to shine at night. God wisely designed the earth so that light helps things live and grow.

117

Sunrise and Sunset

Have you ever watched the sun rise? The sky in the east may turn colors. The whole sky slowly changes from dark to light. Then the sun peeks into view. This time of day is called the sunrise. **Sunrise** is the time the sun appears in the morning.

All morning the sun seems to climb in the sky. Its path takes it toward the west. About noon the sun is high in the sky.

Sunset in the west

During the afternoon, the sun continues its trip west. It becomes lower in the sky. As the sun gets lower, the sky in the west may change colors. **Sunset** is the time the sun disappears in the evening. Then the sky gets darker and night comes.

As all this happens, it looks like the sun moves. But the sun does not really move. It is the earth that is moving!

In what direction does the sun seem to travel during the day?

Noon

Sunrise in the east

A Round Earth

When you look out over a large field or body of water, the earth seems flat. It looks flat because you are seeing only a small part of the earth's surface. When astronauts travel in space, they see the whole earth. They do not see a flat earth. They see that the earth is round like a ball. We call this shape a sphere. We can see pictures of the earth from space. The pictures show that the earth is a sphere.

A globe is a model that can help you learn about the earth and how it moves. It can show you the land and water on the earth's surface. It shows that the earth is tilted. It can help you see how the earth spins. You can use a globe to model how the earth moves in space.

 What is the shape of the earth called?

A Rotating Earth

The earth is always moving in space. One way it moves is that it **rotates,** or spins, like a toy top. Look at the picture of the earth. The arrows show the direction that it spins. It also shows a line going from the North Pole through the center of the earth to the South Pole. This is an imaginary line called the **axis.** The earth rotates on its axis.

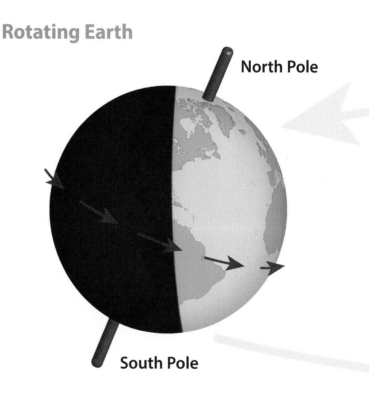

Rotating Earth

North Pole

South Pole

The sun shines in space all the time. As the earth rotates, each part of the earth has daytime and nighttime. Only one side of the earth at a time gets the light from the sun.

It is daytime for the side of the earth that has light. It is nighttime for the side that does not have light.

We measure time by how the earth moves. The earth rotates once every **day**. A day is divided into hours. We have 24 hours in one day. Part of each day is daytime and part is nighttime.

God designed the earth to rotate. Some places are warmed by the sun. Other places where the sun is not shining are cool. If the earth did not rotate, the lit side would become too hot. If the earth did not rotate, the dark side would become too cool. God's wisdom allows people, plants, and animals to survive.

How does the earth move on its axis?

Day and Night Across the World

A globe can help you see how the earth moves. In this activity you will use a globe to show what causes day and night.

Purpose

Observe what causes day and night.

Materials
globe
clay (red, blue, green, and yellow)
flashlight
Activity Manual

Procedure

1. Find the pieces of red, blue, green, and yellow clay on the globe. Record the location of each clay marker in your Activity Manual.

2. Locate the equator on the globe. Darken the room. Pretend your partner is the sun, and have him shine the flashlight at the equator so the light also shines on the red marker.

3. Look at the red and blue markers. Record whether it is daytime or nighttime for each.

4. Slowly rotate the globe while your partner holds the flashlight steady. Stop the globe when the flashlight shines on the blue marker.

5. Look at the red and blue markers. Record whether it is daytime or nighttime for each.

6. Repeat steps 2–5 for the yellow and green markers.

Conclusions

- Did each marker have a daytime and a nighttime?
- What caused some places to be light and others to be dark?

A Revolving Earth

Have you ever ridden a merry-go-round? You may have ridden on a horse or other animal. But you traveled in a circle around the center of the merry-go-round.

The earth also travels around a center. The center is the sun. The earth moves in a path around the sun. We say that the earth **revolves** around the sun. The earth's path around the sun is called an **orbit**.

We measure our years by how long it takes for the earth to revolve around the sun. One complete trip around the sun is a **year**. One year is about 365 days. We divide a year into months and weeks. We use a calendar to show the parts of a year.

Earth Revolving Around the Sun

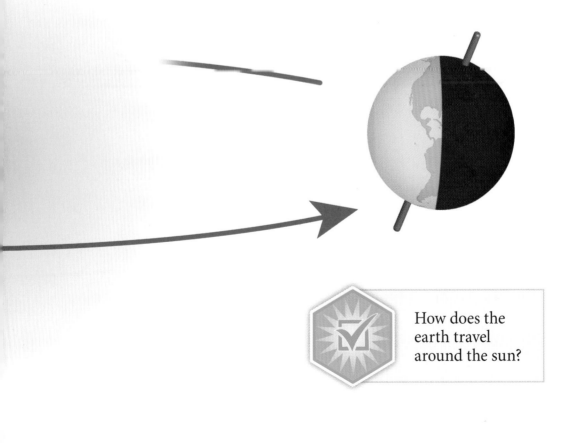

How does the earth travel around the sun?

Seasons

God designed the earth so that it is tilted in space. The earth's axis is not straight up and down.

The earth always tilts in the same direction. This causes some parts of the earth to get more direct sunlight than other parts do.

The parts of the earth that get more sunlight change as the earth revolves around the sun. The earth's orbit and tilt cause the seasons. The four seasons are spring, summer, autumn, and winter.

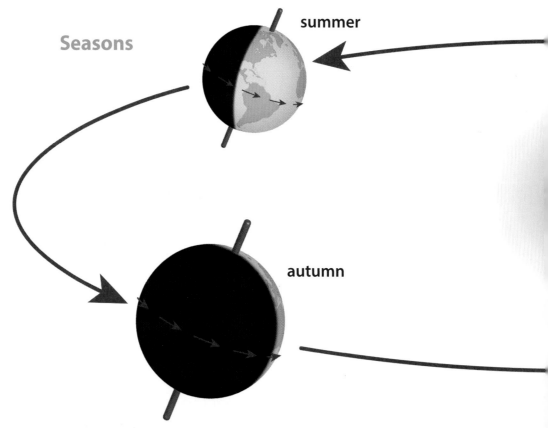

Seasons

summer

autumn

The part of the earth tilted toward the sun gets more sunlight. Where this happens, that part of the earth has summer. At the same time, the other side of the earth is tilted away from the sun. That side gets less sunlight and has winter.

God said in Genesis 8:22 that there would be summer and winter. He also said there would be seedtime and harvest. God designed the earth to be tilted and to revolve to cause the seasons.

spring

winter

What causes the earth to have seasons?

9 How Light Works

How can we use light?

The Bible tells us in Genesis 1 that God created light. He spoke, and there was light. He divided the light and darkness so that we have daytime and nighttime.

In the daytime we can see the sun. God created the sun to give light to the earth. **Light** is a form of energy. People, animals, and plants need light to live and grow. Studying light helps us use it well. In this chapter, look for different ways people use light.

Sources of Light

The sun is a source of light. This means that the sun makes its own light. But there are other sources of light. Some sources are natural, like fire. Other sources are manmade, like light bulbs.

God made the sun and the stars as sources of light. He also gave people the ability and resources to make tools to give us light. Manmade sources of light include candles, lamps, and flashlights.

What are some sources of light?

133

How Light Moves

Most objects do not make their own light. You see the objects because light shines on them.

Light travels in a straight line. When it hits an object, the light bounces off the object in another direction. The object **reflects** the light. Your eyes see the light that reflects off the object. Shiny, smooth objects, such as mirrors, reflect light very well.

You need light to see. Light lets you observe the world around you. It lets you see what color things are.

Since light is energy, most kinds of light also give off heat. Sunlight helps warm the earth. You can feel warmth from a campfire or fireplace. Some light bulbs also give off heat. People, animals, and plants need light and warmth to live.

 How does light travel?

Colors in Light

A beam of light from a flashlight or another source appears white. But light is not really white. Light is made of many colors.

A rainbow shows the colors in light. Sunlight shines through the raindrops in the air. The raindrops bend the light so we can see the colors. The colors of a rainbow are red, orange, yellow, green, blue, indigo, and violet.

During the Flood, it rained for many days. Water covered the whole earth. After the Flood, God made a promise. He said that He would never again cover all the earth with water. He put a rainbow in the sky. Every rainbow reminds us that God keeps His promises.

We see objects because light reflects off them. Lighter-colored objects reflect more light. We can see them better. Light colors also are cooler. They reflect some of the light's energy.

Dark colors take in, or **absorb**, light. They are harder to see. They also are warmer. They absorb energy instead of reflecting it.

Health and Safety

When you ride your bike or walk along a road, think about the clothes you wear. Wearing dark clothes can put your safety at risk. Bright colors help you be seen in the daytime. Wearing something reflective is best at night.

 What kinds of colors reflect more light?

Light and Objects

Light moves in a straight line until it shines on something. Light can shine through some objects. Anything that allows most light to shine through it is **transparent**.

Air and water are transparent. They let light shine through them. Clear plastic and windows also let light shine through.

Transparent

Some objects allow only some light to shine through. Some light can shine through tissue paper, but some is blocked. This also happens when you shine light through a piece of notebook paper or wax paper. Anything that allows only some light to shine through is **translucent**.

Some objects block all light. Light cannot shine through a book or a person. Anything that does not allow any light to shine through is **opaque**.

Translucent   Opaque

What kind of object lets most light shine through it?

Observing Light

You have been learning about light and how it travels. It can travel through some things and reflect off others.

In this activity you will be using your observation skills. You will classify objects that are transparent, translucent, or opaque.

Purpose

Classify objects as transparent, translucent, or opaque.

Materials
Activity Manual

Procedure

1. Explore inside and outside to find 8 objects to classify as transparent, translucent, or opaque.

2. List each object in your Activity Manual. You may draw pictures of objects if you do not know their names.

3. Mark whether each object is transparent, translucent, or opaque.

4. Describe why you classified each object as you did.

5. Graph the number of objects you found in each classification. Share your results.

Conclusions

- Why did you classify each object as transparent, translucent, or opaque?

- Which kind of objects did you find the most of?

Shadows

When something blocks light, a **shadow** forms. The light source is on one side of the object. A shadow forms on the opposite side.

Shine a light on the right side of an object. The shadow forms on the left side. Move the light to the left side. The shadow now forms on the right side of the object. The place where the shadow forms depends on where the light is.

The shadow forms on the opposite side of the object from the light.

A shadow has a shape much like the object that blocks the light. But it is not always the same size. By moving the light source, you can change the size of the shadow. You can also change the size of the shadow by moving the object.

The shadow is smaller when the object is farther from the lamp.

The shadow is larger when the object is closer to the lamp.

 What are two ways to change a shadow's size?

The Sun and Shadows

When you are outside on a sunny day, you can watch shadows change. They change as the sun appears to move across the sky.

In the morning the sun is low in the sky toward the east. This causes long shadows. At noon, the sun is high above in the sky. Shadows are very short. By evening, the sun is low in the sky in the west. The shadows are long again. But they are in a different position from where they were in the morning.

Science and the Bible

Shadows always move a certain way as the sun moves across the sky. But the Bible tells us of one time a shadow moved the opposite way. God moved the sun so that the shadow moved backward. God did this as a sign that He would heal King Hezekiah of Judah.

Evening   Noon   Morning

When during the day is your shadow the shortest?

Shadow Puppets

You can tell a story with light and shadows.
Choose a short story you know or make one up.
Then write the story like a play and make some puppets to
help you tell it.

What to Do

1. Work with some friends to write a script for two or
   three characters.
2. Draw your characters and cut them out.
3. Tape a craft stick to each to make a puppet.
4. Tell your story with the stage and light your teacher
   provides.

145

10 How Matter Changes

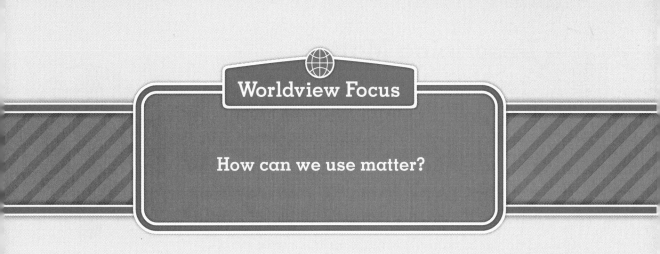
Look around you. Everything you see is made of matter. **Matter** is anything that has mass and takes up space. The clothes you wear are matter. The pencil you use is matter. The water you drink and the air you breathe are matter. The sun and planets are made of matter too. When we work with God's world, we work with matter.

Describing Matter

Matter has mass. **Mass** is the amount of matter in an object. You can measure mass with a balance.

A heavier object contains more matter. It has more mass than a lighter object does. A basketball and a beach ball are about the same size. But a basketball is heavier than a beach ball. The material that the basketball is made of has more mass.

Matter also takes up space. When a bucket is filled with water, there is no room for other matter, such as shells. If you drop shells into the bucket, the water will start to flow over the edge. The water and the shells are both matter. They both take up space. In order to use matter in better ways, you need to understand it.

Forms of Matter

Matter has three forms. It can be a solid, liquid, or gas. Your clothes and books are solids. Water is a liquid. The air you breathe is a gas.

Solids

Solid is one form of matter. A solid has mass. It takes up space. But unlike other forms of matter, a solid keeps its own shape. A solid also keeps its own size.

Most of the things you see around you are solids. A solid can be hard like an ice cube. A solid can be soft like a towel.

Solid
Shape stays the same
Size stays the same

What is mass?

Liquids

Liquid is another form of matter. A liquid has mass. It takes up space. But a liquid does not have its own shape. It changes shape to fit whatever container it is in. Its size, or amount, does not change.

The shape of some paint can change to fit its container. But the amount of the paint does not change. The amount of a liquid stays the same when its shape changes.

Milk is a liquid. Juice is a liquid. Honey and glue are also liquids. Each of these liquids takes the shape of the container that it is in.

Liquid
Changes shape to fit its container
Size stays the same

Gases

Gas is also a form of matter. A gas has mass. But a gas is different from both a solid and a liquid. A gas can change both its shape and its size. Gases are the only kind of matter that always fill their containers.

Air is a gas. When you breathe out air, you do not see it. But if you blow into a beach ball, you can see the beach ball change shape and size. The air fills the ball. Even when the ball seems to be full of air, you often can still blow a little more air into it.

Gas
Changes shape to fit its container
Changes size to fill its container

Which form of matter can change both its shape and its size?

Changes to Matter

Matter has three forms: solid, liquid, and gas. Sometimes matter changes from one form to another. Adding heat to an object can make it change form. Removing heat from an object can also make it change form. We can use matter better when we understand how it changes. Knowing how matter changes can help us use it wisely.

Solids to Liquids

Heating a solid can make it change to a liquid. We say that the solid melts. You can melt butter in a pan on the stove. Butter can also melt if you leave it in bright sunshine. But the butter does not melt as quickly in the sunshine as it does on the stove.

Most candles are made of wax. They are solids at room temperature. But when a candle is lit, it starts to melt. The heat from the flame causes the solid wax to change to a liquid. The liquid runs down the side of the candle.

A solid changes to a liquid when heat is added.

Some solids are easier to melt than others. Things like butter and wax melt easily. Other solids, such as metals, do not melt easily. Metals have to be heated to very high temperatures before they melt. A kitchen stove is not hot enough to melt most metals. That's why metal pans can be used for cooking.

Ice is a solid that can be easy to melt. During the winter, the water in birdbaths and bowls for outside pets may freeze. To change a solid to a liquid, we know we can use heat. We can heat water and pour the warm water on the ice to melt it. Water pipes can also freeze during cold winter nights. We again can use heat by wrapping the pipes with insulation or other warm materials.

A solid has its own shape. But when it melts, it becomes a liquid. As a liquid, its shape can change.

 What happens to a solid when heat is added?

Liquids to Gases

Liquids can also change when they are heated. When you add heat to a liquid, it changes to a gas. You have seen this happen with water.

When it rains, the rain often forms puddles. When the sun comes out, the puddles dry up. What happens to the water? The heat from the sun causes the liquid to change to a gas. We say the liquid evaporates.

You cannot see the evaporated water, but it is in the air. The gas that forms from water is called water vapor.

A liquid changes to a gas when it is heated.

Heating water on a stove can cause the water to boil. As the water boils, the amount of water in the pan becomes less. The water that left the pan has evaporated and become water vapor.

What can happen to a liquid when it is heated?

Gases to Liquids

Matter can change form when it is heated. Matter can also change form when heat is removed and it is cooled. Cooling a gas can change it to a liquid. When a gas changes to a liquid, we say the gas condenses.

Suppose you put some cold water into a glass. Later you notice little water droplets on the outside of the glass. The cold glass cooled the air touching it. It cooled some of the water vapor in the air. The water vapor condensed and became drops of liquid.

Creation Corner

Water vapor is in the air all around you. When the air becomes cool, the water vapor is also cooled. It forms droplets of water. Often the droplets form clouds. As clouds cool, the droplets join to form larger drops. When the drops are big enough, gravity pulls them toward the earth as rain. Rain is condensation. God provides water for many areas of the earth with rain.

Water vapor touching the cool window glass changes to a liquid.

Liquids to Solids

Liquids can change when they are cooled. Cooling a liquid makes it change to a solid. We say that the liquid freezes.

Juice is a liquid. But when it is poured into a container and put into the freezer, it changes. The freezer cools the juice. The liquid juice changes into a solid frozen treat!

You may not think the wax of a candle freezes, but it does. The hot, melted wax drips down the side of the candle as a liquid. It moves away from the heat of the flame. It cools and changes back to a solid. This form of the wax is frozen.

The frozen treat is a liquid that has been cooled to become a solid.

What happens to a gas when it is cooled?

Changing a Solid

When solids are heated they change. Some solids change at room temperature. Others must be heated a little more. Some change only at very high temperatures.

Your hands are warm. You will use the heat from your hands to try to change some solids.

Problem

Which solid will change fastest when heated?

Materials
metric measuring cups
3 sealable bags
chocolate chips
crayon pieces
ice pieces
Activity Manual

Procedure

1. Predict which solid you think will change first when heat is added. Complete the hypothesis in your Activity Manual.

2. Measure 100 mL of each solid. Place each in a sealable bag.

3. Describe how you think each will change when heat is added.

4. Choose one bag and give the others to your partners.

5. Write the starting time. At the same time, all of you hold and rub your solids between your hands.

6. Observe and write the time when one solid has completely changed.

7. Record which changed first.

8. Observe and write a description for each.

Conclusions

- Which completely changed first?
- How did it change when heat was added?
- How can you use what you learned to change it back to a solid?

Temperature

Matter can change as heat is added or removed. Some kinds of matter change only when they are very hot. Gold melts at a very hot temperature. Other kinds of matter freeze only when they are very cold. Salt water in the ocean freezes at a very low temperature.

We use a thermometer to measure temperature. Matter that is hot has higher temperatures. Matter that is cold has lower temperatures.

People have found ways to change temperatures. When you put an apple in a refrigerator, the apple gets colder. Its temperature goes down. When you bake a pie in an oven, the pie gets warmer. Its temperature goes up.

When the water is cooled, the temperature goes down.

When the water is heated, the temperature goes up.

Working with God's World

God planned our whole world. He made all matter. He designed matter so that it can change. If we did not understand how matter changes, we could not use it to do many things.

Every day you use matter. You eat solids. You drink liquids. Sometimes you change matter, such as when you make ice. Learning how matter works is part of learning to work with God's world. Working with God's world is one way you can please Him.

 How does the temperature change when something is heated or cooled?

11

How Things Move

A train engine hauls loaded cars down the track. A bulldozer clears dirt for a house. A kite sails high in the sky. Children push each other on swings. The train cars, dirt, kite, and swings are all moving. They all moved because of either a push or a pull.

163

Force

God created people to work with His creation. When you push an object, you cause it to move away from you. When you pull an object, you cause it to move toward you. A **force** is a push or a pull. You use a force to make something move. People use forces to work with God's creation.

Without force, matter will not move. A train's cars will stay still unless a force moves them. Dirt forms a pile unless a force moves it. A kite will not fly and swings cannot move without forces to move them.

Not all forces are the same. A stronger force causes an object to go faster and farther. A stronger kick causes a ball to go faster and farther than a lighter kick does. A strong wind moves a sailboat faster than a gentle breeze does.

Sometimes we do not need to move something farther or faster. Sometimes we need to move something that is heavy. It takes more force to move a heavier object. You can easily carry a glass of milk. It takes a lot more force to carry a gallon of milk.

What is a force?

Motion

When a toy car rolls across the floor, we say that it is in motion. **Motion** happens when an object moves. A force causes an object's motion. The toy car may be pushed or pulled. That force causes the car to move.

A force can change the direction of an object's motion. A soccer player changes the direction of a rolling soccer ball when he passes to another player. When he kicks the ball from the left, it goes to the right. If he kicks it from the right, it goes left.

What causes an object's motion?

• Meet the Scientist • Sir Isaac Newton

Sir Isaac Newton was a scientist who lived long ago. He was interested in motion. He came up with ideas that describe how things move. He tested his ideas. Today his ideas are called Newton's laws of motion.

Forces Walk

Things are in motion all around you. Can you see the hand on the clock move? Maybe you see someone sharpening a pencil. Everything that moves has a force that is pushing or pulling it. Go for a walk and observe the objects that are moving.

What to Do

1. Get your Activity Manual page and a pencil.
2. Go for a walk.
3. Look for things that are in motion. List them in your Activity Manual.
4. Mark the kind of force that you think is causing each to move.
5. Share your observations with others.

Kinds of Forces

Every day people use different kinds of forces to do work. Knowing about the different kinds of forces can help us use them better.

Friction

A force can cause an object to move. It can also cause it to stop moving. **Friction** is a force that slows down or stops motion.

Friction happens when surfaces touch each other. Rough surfaces cause more friction. Smooth surfaces cause less friction.

Friction can be helpful. The brakes on a car use friction to stop the car from moving. Friction also helps keep your feet from sliding on the ground when you walk.

Spreading sand on the ice causes friction.

If there is not enough friction, there are ways to make more. By making a surface rougher, you can cause more friction. Perhaps you have tried to walk on ice. Ice is smooth. It has very little friction and is hard to walk on. Putting sand on the ice makes it less slippery. The sand causes friction. Wearing boots with a rough surface on the bottom can also cause friction to keep you from slipping.

Friction wears out the soles of shoes.

At times friction can cause problems. Friction causes hinges on doors to creak and stick. Friction wears out socks and the soles of shoes.

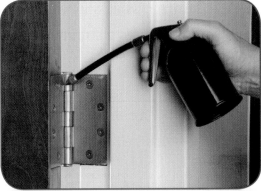

Oiling a hinge reduces friction.

If there is too much friction, you can sometimes make less. By making a surface smoother, you can reduce friction. Oil is put on hinges to make them move without creaking and sticking.

What is friction?

Gravity

If you were to drop a ball, how would you expect it to move? You would not expect it to move toward the sky. You expect it to fall toward the earth. A force pulls it to the earth. **Gravity** is the force that pulls all things toward the center of the earth.

Gravity holds you to the ground when you stand. You can jump off the ground. But gravity pulls you back down. You can throw a ball up into the air. But gravity pulls it back down. A sled slides down a hill because of gravity. Gravity also causes a stream to flow downhill.

Gravity pulls the jumpers back to the earth.

If something has more mass, gravity has a greater pull on it. We say that the object is heavy. Gravity has less pull on something with less mass. We say that the object is light.

The pull of gravity on an object can be measured. **Weight** is the measure of the force of gravity on an object. People use a scale to weigh objects. The greater the amount of pull, the more an object weighs.

The scale shows the weight of the apples.

What is gravity?

Magnetic Attraction

Magnets can stick to some things. But there are many things that do not stick to a magnet.

In this activity you will predict whether a magnet will stick to each object. Then you will test your predictions.

Problem

Which items are attracted to a magnet?

Procedure

1. Choose 10 objects to test. Write the names of the objects on the chart in your Activity Manual.

2. Examine each object. Describe what it is made of in the chart.

3. Circle whether or not you expect each object to stick to the magnet.

4. Place all the objects in a paper bag.

5. Place the magnet inside the bag and gently shake the bag.

6. Pull out the magnet. Observe the objects that stuck to it. On the chart, circle "Yes" for the objects that stuck to the magnet.

> **Materials**
> plastic button
> eraser
> nail
> metal paper clip
> penny
> staples
> 4 other objects
> small paper bag
> magnet
> Activity Manual

7. Repeat steps 4–5 until there are no objects left in the bag that stick to the magnet.

8. Remove any remaining objects from the bag. On the chart, circle "No" for the objects that did not stick to the magnet.

Conclusions

- Did your results match your predictions?
- What can you summarize about the objects that stuck to the magnet?
- How can you classify the objects you put in the bag?
- How can you use what you learned about magnetic objects?

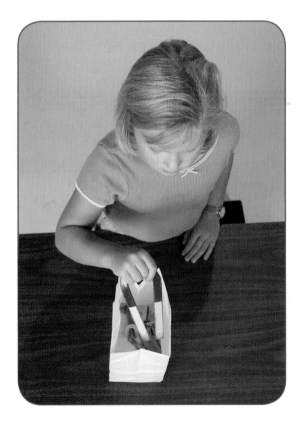

Magnetism

Magnets are objects that can cause a force. They can push or pull certain metal objects without touching them. The force of a magnet is called **magnetism**.

Magnets come in many sizes and shapes. They may be bars, discs, or curved like a horseshoe.

Some areas of a magnet have stronger magnetism than other areas. The areas of a magnet that have the strongest magnetism are called the poles.

Magnets have two poles. They are called the north and south poles. On a bar magnet the poles are labeled *S* for south and *N* for north.

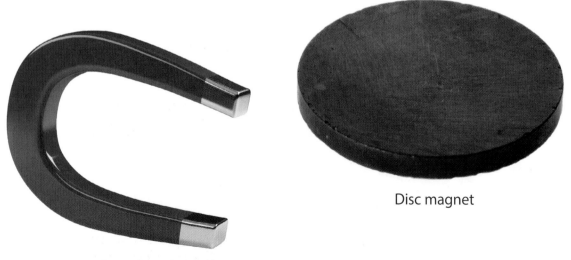

Horseshoe magnet

Disc magnet

Have you ever tried to put the north poles of two magnets together? No matter how hard you try, poles that are the same will not stick to each other. Like poles repel, or push away from, each other.

If you put a north pole and a south pole close to each other, they will stick to each other. Opposite poles attract, or pull toward, each other.

Repelling and Attracting

Like poles repel, or push away from, each other.

Opposite poles attract, or pull toward, each other.

God created the forces in our world. Learning about these forces can help you do your work well. Doing your work well is one way to glorify God.

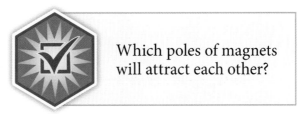

Which poles of magnets will attract each other?

12

How the Body Works

God made the parts of your body. He planned each part to work the way it does. Each part has a special job of its own. The parts also work together in groups called systems. A **system** is a group of parts that work together to do a job. We study these systems so we can stay healthy.

177

The Skeletal System

All the bones in your body work together in the **skeletal system**. Your **bones** are hard parts of your body. You may have seen old, dry bones in a museum. Those bones are dead, but the bones inside your body are alive. They grow and change. They make new bone.

God gave your bones some important jobs. One job is to give your body support. Your skeleton is the frame of bones that supports your body and gives it shape.

Your bones also protect the soft parts inside your body. In your head, your skull protects your brain. In your chest are flat, curved bones called ribs. The ribs surround most of your chest. They form your rib cage. Your heart, lungs, and stomach are protected by your rib cage.

Your bones have a third job. They allow your body to move. Sets of bones form joints that allow your arms and legs to move. If you bend forward, you can feel bumps down the center of your back. Each bump is a bone. This set of bones is your spine. It starts at the top of your neck and ends below your waist. Your spine allows your body to twist and bend.

Spine

Skeletal System

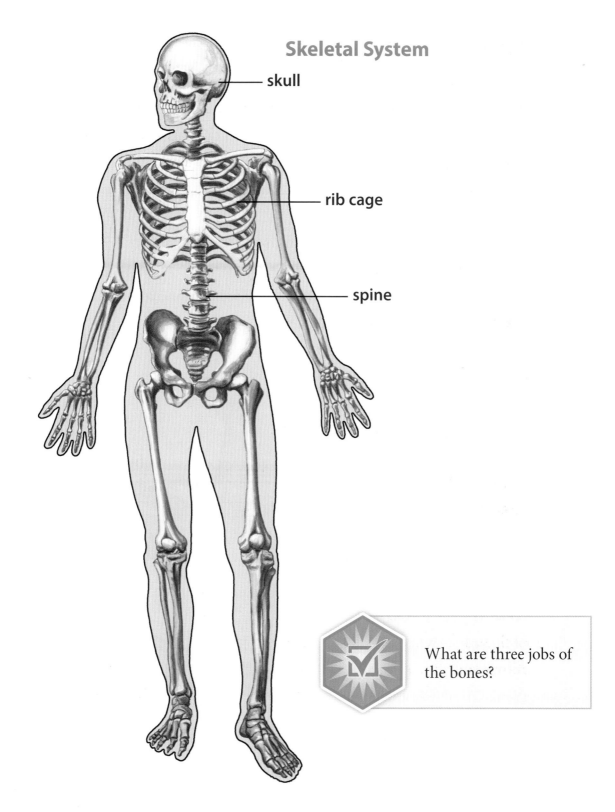

skull

rib cage

spine

What are three jobs of the bones?

The Muscular System

Your skeleton supports and protects your body. It allows your body to move. But it cannot move on its own. All the muscles in your body work together in the **muscular system**. God designed the muscular system to work with the skeletal system. Your **muscles** make the bones and other body parts move.

Some muscles are small. The muscles that move your eyes are very small. Other muscles are large. The muscles in the top of your legs are very large. They work to move large bones so you can walk, run, and stand.

Many of your muscles connect to bones. When the muscles move, they move your bones. You control these muscles by thinking about moving them. They move when and how you choose.

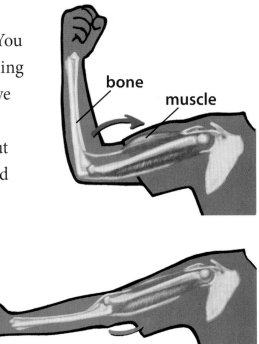

bone

muscle

Some muscles move without your thinking about them. God made muscles that work even while you sleep. Your heart is this kind of muscle. It works all the time whether you think about it or not.

Your bones and muscles are tough. God made them that way so you can use them for work and play. You can keep them strong by eating heathy food and exercising. When you play sports, you should wear protective gear. The gear helps protect your bones and muscles.

Muscular System

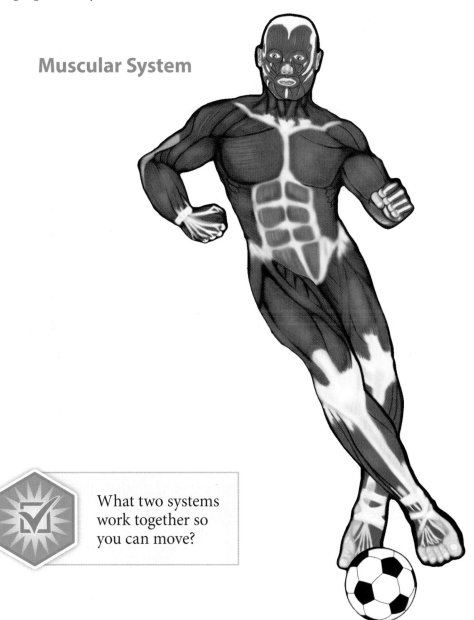

What two systems work together so you can move?

The Circulatory System

Your heart and blood vessels work together to form the **circulatory system**. This system has the job of moving blood to all parts of your body. Your blood moves through **blood vessels**. These tubes take the blood to your eyes, fingers, toes, and everywhere in between.

Your blood carries oxygen and nutrients that your body needs to live. Blood also carries wastes to be removed from your body.

Circulatory System

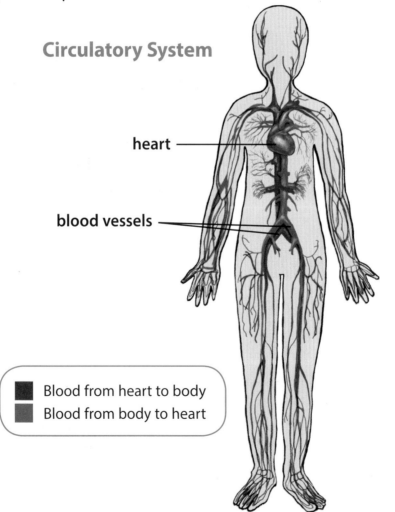

heart

blood vessels

Blood from heart to body
Blood from body to heart

Your **heart** is a powerful muscle. Each time your heart beats, it pumps blood through the body. It beats all the time. The only rest your heart gets is between beats.

Your heart muscle is about the size of your fist. As you grow, so does your heart. When you are an adult, your heart will be about the size of your adult fist.

Heart Size

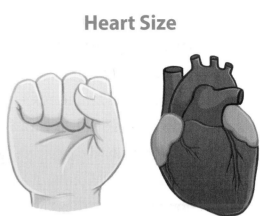

A doctor uses a stethoscope to listen to your heart.

A trip to the doctor helps you to stay healthy. A doctor listens to your heart. He will listen for a "lubb-dubb" sound. That is the sound a healthy heart makes as it beats.

A doctor wants to know your heart rate. Your heart rate is how fast your heart is pumping. When you exercise, your heart rate gets faster. When you rest, your heart rate slows.

What is the job of the circulatory system?

The Respiratory System

Every living thing needs oxygen to live. Oxygen is in the air around you. Your **respiratory system** helps your body get the oxygen it needs from the air.

You have two lungs in your chest. Your **lungs** fill with air when you breathe in. They empty when you breathe out. The muscle that causes them to move is called the diaphragm. When you breathe in, your diaphragm pulls down and makes room for your lungs to fill with fresh air. When you breathe out, your diaphragm muscle pushes up. This pushes the old air out of your lungs.

Respiratory System

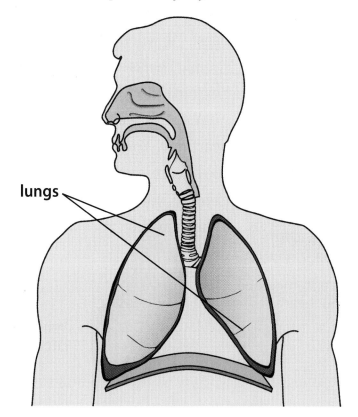

lungs

Your respiratory system works with your circulatory system. The heart pumps blood to your lungs. There the blood picks up oxygen. The blood vessels carry the oxygen to all the parts of your body.

Air to the Heart

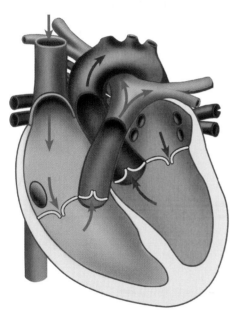

Blood from heart to body
Blood from body to heart

Once your body uses the oxygen, other blood vessels carry the blood back to your heart. The cycle starts again.

You breathe about 20 times every minute. Exercise is a good way to help your heart and lungs stay strong.

How does oxygen get inside the body?

The Digestive System

Your meals are some of the most important times in your day. The food you eat provides the nutrients your body needs to live and grow.

Remember that your blood carries nutrients. But it cannot carry whole bites of meat or vegetables. The foods you eat must be broken down. That is the job of your digestive system. The parts of your **digestive system** work together. They break down food so your body can use it.

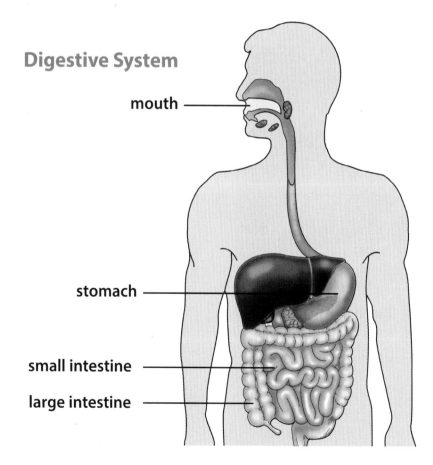

Digestive System

mouth

stomach

small intestine

large intestine

Your food starts to digest, or break down, in your mouth. Your teeth chew and break up the food. Saliva is the liquid in your mouth. The saliva softens and starts to digest the food.

When you swallow, your food travels down a tube to your stomach. Your **stomach** is a bag made of muscle. The muscles work to squeeze and mix the food with digestive juices. The juices help break down the food even more. Your food is a thick liquid when it leaves the stomach.

The liquid then moves to your small intestine. Your small intestine is a very long tube with thin walls. By now the nutrients are small enough to pass through the walls. They move into the nearby blood vessels. There the blood carries the nutrients to feed the other parts of the body.

Not all the food you eat is used by your body. The food that cannot be used moves on to the large intestine. After a while, the body gets rid of the unused food.

 What is another word for breaking down food?

Food and Exercise

You need food to grow and be healthy. Food is divided into groups. You should eat some of each group every day. But you need to eat more of some groups than of others.

Fruits and vegetables are full of vitamins and minerals your body needs. A healthy meal plan includes lots of fruits and vegetables.

Dairy products are also very important. Your body is growing. Milk and foods made from milk have nutrients that help build strong bones and muscles.

Protein is a nutrient that your body needs. It helps your body work properly. Foods in the protein group include fish, chicken, beef, eggs, beans, and nuts.

Grains are seeds such as wheat, rice, and corn. Foods made from grains include cereal, bread, and pasta. Grains have many nutrients. They also help your body digest the foods you eat.

Eating healthy food and drinking milk help build a strong body.

You also need to exercise to be strong and healthy. Exercise makes your heart and other muscles stronger. It also helps your bones get stronger.

You should get about one hour of exercise every day. Riding your bike is one way to get exercise. Playing sports is also a way to get exercise.

God made your body. He planned all the systems to work together. The Bible tells us that a Christian should use his body to glorify God. Taking care of your body is a way to glorify God.

Exercise each day to help build a strong body.

What are two ways to help build a strong body?

Mapping My Body

Maps help us know where things are. Different kinds of maps show different things. Many maps show roads. Other maps show buildings. Some maps even show where stars are in the sky. In this activity you will make a map of some systems of your body.

Purpose

Make a map of some body systems.

Procedure

1. Lie flat on a large sheet of paper. Ask your partner to trace the outline of your body.

2. Use the diagrams of the body systems from this chapter to help you place and label the parts.

3. On a piece of construction paper, draw a heart. Remember to make it about the size of your fist. Cut it out and glue it to your map. Label the heart.

4. Use red yarn to show blood vessels that take blood to all parts of the body. Use blue yarn to show the blood vessels that bring blood back to the heart.

Materials
large sheet of paper
construction paper
scissors
glue
yarn (red and blue)
heart shape
two lung shapes
stomach shape
crayons or markers

5. Cut out the lung shapes and glue them to your map. Label the shapes.

6. Cut out the stomach shape and glue it to your map. Label the shape.

7. Draw a face on your map. Add hair.

8. Draw a tube from the stomach to the mouth.

9. Add details that you choose from other body systems.

10. Use your map to tell others about the body systems. Tell what you can do to keep your body healthy.

Conclusions

- What systems are shown on your map?
- What are ways you can keep your heart and lungs healthy?

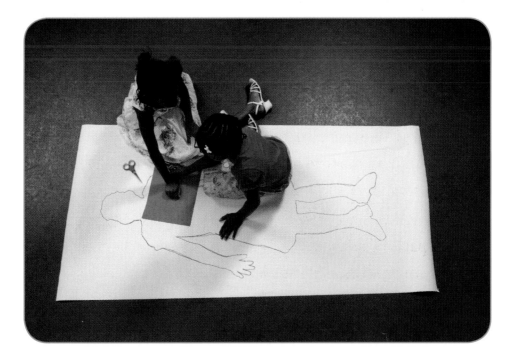

Glossary

A

absorb—To take in.

axis—An imaginary line through the earth.

B

blood vessels—Tubes that carry blood to all parts of the body.

bone—The hard parts of your body.

C

circulatory system—The system that moves blood to all parts of the body.

community—All the living things in one area.

conserve—To not waste.

core—The center layer of the earth; inner core believed to be made of iron.

Creation—The belief that God spoke and made all things.

crust—The outside layer of the earth; made of rock.

Layers of the Earth

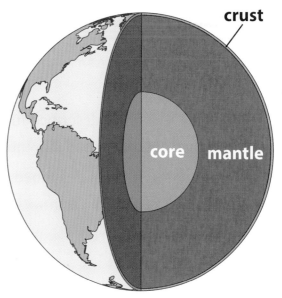

crust

core   mantle

D

day—The time that the earth takes to rotate once.

digestive system—The system that breaks down food so your body can use it.

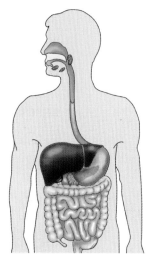

Digestive system

E

earthquake—When large areas of the earth's surface shake and move.

energy—What is needed to cause change.

environment—All the nonliving things that are around a living thing.

erosion—The moving of soil from one place to another.

evolution—The belief that all things came about by chance.

experiment—A scientific test to solve a problem.

extinct—When none of the animals of a certain kind are still alive.

F

Fall—The event described in Genesis 3 when the first man sinned and brought death into the world.

Flood—The event described in Genesis 6–9 when God covered the entire earth with water.

flower—The part of the plant that makes seeds.

force—A push or a pull.

fossil—The remains of a living thing that died long ago.

fossil fuels—Natural resources formed when plants and animals are buried quickly.

friction—A force that slows down or stops motion.

G

gas—The form of matter that changes shape and size to fill its container.

gravity—The force that pulls all things toward the center of the earth.

H

habitat—A place where a living thing lives and can find food, water, and shelter.

heart—The powerful muscle that pumps blood through the body.

L

lava—Melted rock that comes out of a volcano.

leaves—The part of a plant that makes food for the plant.

life cycle—All the stages of the life of a living thing.

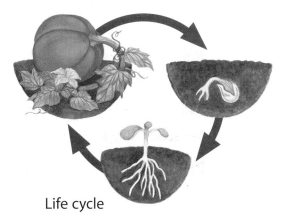

Life cycle

light—A form of energy that people need in order to see.

liquid—The form of matter that changes shape to fit its container while its size, or amount, stays the same.

living—Things that need food, water, and air to live and grow.

lungs—The body parts that fill with air when you breathe in.

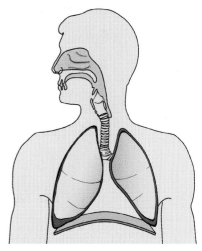

Lungs

M

magnetism—The force of a magnet.

mantle—The layer of the earth under the crust; made of melted rock.

mass—The amount of matter in an object.

matter—Anything that has mass and takes up space.

motion—What happens when an object moves.

muscle—Makes the bones and other body parts move.

muscular system—The system of muscles in the body.

N

natural resource—A material in nature that God made for people's use.

need—What a living thing must have to stay alive.

nonliving—Things that do not need food, water, and air and do not grow.

nutrient—Things found in food that are needed for life.

O

opaque—Anything that does not allow any light to shine through it.

orbit—The earth's path around the sun.

Orbit

P

pollution—Anything that makes the air, water, or land dirty.

population—All the living things of one kind that live in one area.

process—Ordered steps.

R

recycle—To make something new out of an object.

Redemption—Christ's work of rescuing everything that is damaged by sin.

reduce—To use less of something.

reflect—When light bounces off an object.

respiratory system—The system that helps your body get the oxygen it needs from the air.

reuse—To use something again.

revolve—The movement of the earth in a path around the sun.

roots—The part of the plant that takes in water and nutrients from the soil; these help hold plants in the ground.

rotate—To spin.

S

science process skill—A skill that helps scientists gather and use information.

seedling—A young plant.

seismograph—A machine that records the earth's movements.

shadow—A dark area formed when an object blocks light.

Seedling

shelter—A safe place to live.

skeletal system—The system of bones in the body.

solid—The form of matter that keeps its own shape and size.

stem—The part of the plant that moves water and nutrients from roots to leaves; holds plant upright.

stomach—The bag of muscle that digests swallowed food.

sunrise—The time the sun appears in the morning.

sunset—The time the sun goes down in the evening.

system—A group of parts that work together to do a job.

T

translucent—Anything that allows some light to shine through it.

transparent—Anything that allows most light to shine through it.

V

volcano—An opening in the earth's crust that allows lava (melted rock) to flow out.

W

weight—The measure of the force of gravity on an object.

worldview—A way of looking at or understanding the world.

Y

year—One trip of the earth around the sun; 365 days.

Index

nonliving, 23

nutrient, 42, 182, 186, 188

O

opaque, 139

orbit, 127

P

plant parts, 42–43

pollution, 109

population, 54

process, 14

R

rainbow, 136

recycle, 112–113

redemption, 2

reduce, 111

reflect, 134

respiratory system, 184–185

reuse, 110

revolve, 127

rib cage, 178

roots, 42

rotate, 122

S

science process skills, 6–10

    classify, 8

    communicate, 10

    infer, 9

    measure, 9

    observe, 7

    predict, 10

scientists, 5–17

    Cousteau, Jacques-Yves, 104

    de Mestral, George, 48

    Newton, Isaac, 166

seasons, 128–129

seedling, 45

seeds, 47–49

seismograph, 101

shadow, 142–144

shelter, 28

skeletal system, 178

skull, 178

solid, 149

spine, 178

Stegosaurus, 81

stem, 43

stomach, 187

sunrise, 118

sunset, 119

system, 177

Photo Credits

Key: (t) top; (c) center;
(b) bottom; (l) left; (r) right;
(bg) background; (i) inset

Cover
© iStock.com/FabioFilzi

Chapter 1

4 Destinations RM | Brian Guzzetti/Media Bakery; **6l, 7tl** © 2009 JupiterImages Corporation; **6r** SW Productions /Photodisc/Getty Images; **7tr** © iStockphoto.com/izabela Habur; **7b** © iStock.com/Paha_L; **8** eZeePics Studio/Bigstock .com; **9t** BJU Photo Services; **9b** kazoka/Shutterstock.com; **10t, 10b, 12b, 14 –17 all, 19** Unusual Films; **11** Media Bakery; **12t** © piai - Fotolia.com; **13t** OHAUS Corporation; **13b** © 2008 JupiterImages Corporation

Chapter 2

20 JoeFotoSS/Shutterstock.com; **22–23** © Patti McConville/Alamy Stock Photo; **24t, 25l, 29tl** © JupiterImages Corporation; **24b** PhotoDisc, Inc.; **25r** © 2009 JupiterImages Corporation; **27** Unusual Films; **28** © iStock.com /JimSchemel; **29tr** Carlos Arranz Pena © Fotolia; **29b** Robert Cable/Photographer's Choice RF/Getty Images; **30** all Goodman Photography; **31** © iStock.com/jimveilleux; **31i** © iStock.com/yenwen; **32** © 2009 JupiterImages Corporation; **32i** 2009 JupiterImages Corporation; **33l** Copyright © Kenneth H. Thomas/Photo Researchers, Inc.; **33r** Frans Lanting/Mint Images/Getty Images; **34** © Richard Nelson/123RF; **35t** © Victoria L. Almgren|Dreamstime .com; **35b** cpaulfell/Shutterstock.com

Chapter 3

38 © iStock.com/Ugurhan Betin; **40–41** JacobH/iStockphoto/Getty Images; **42–43** Neil Fletcher/Dorling Kindersley /Getty Images; **47 all** © 2009 JupiterImages Corporation; **48** kathyclark777/iStockphoto/Getty Images; **49l** Steve Byland © Fotolia.com; **49r** John E Marriott/All Canada Photos/SuperStock; **51** BJU Photo Services

Chapter 4

52 argovcom/iStock/Getty Images Plus/Getty Images; **58–59** bg © Neale Clark/robertharding/Corbis; **58l** © Ralph Schmaelter/**123**RF; **58r, 60i, 64r** © 2009 JupiterImages Corporation; **59** © iStock.com/jamesbenet; **60bg** © iStock .com/AustralianCamera; **61bg** © iStockphoto.com/Laila Roberg; **61i** © iStockphoto.com/John Pitcher; **62–63bg** © iStockphoto.com/George Olsson; **62i** © iStockphoto.com/James Brey; **63i** © iStockphoto.com/Canon_Bob; **64–65bg** © Papo - Fotolia.com; **64l** © iStock.com/paule858; **65l** Dante Fenolio/Science Source/Getty Images; **65r** © iStockphoto .com/strmko; **66–67bg** Elena Elisseeva/Shutterstock.com; **66i** © iStock.com/fenkep; **67i** raymond brown - Fotolia.com; **69** Unusual Films

Chapter 5

70 Jason Edwards/Media Bakery; **72–73** © iStockphoto.com/SoopySue; **75** © iStockphoto.com/digital94086; **76t** DEA /L. ROMANO/De Agostini/Getty Images; **76b** ribeiroantonio/Shutterstock.com; **77t** Colin Keates/Dorling Kindersley /Getty Images; **77b** Reimar/Shutterstock.com; **78–79** Puwadol Jaturawutthichai/Shutterstock.com; **80** David McNew /Getty Images Sport/Getty Images; **82** blickwinkel/Alamy Stock Photo; **85** Unusual Films

Chapter 6

86 Ron Dahlquist/Media Bakery; **91tl** © iStock.com/BeholdingEye; **91tr** © iStock.com/ Łukasz Kurbiel; **91bg** © iStock .com/Brian Raisbeck; **92** Carsten Peter/Speleoresearch & Films/National Geographic/Getty Images; **93** PhotoDisc, Inc.; **97** Unusual Films; **98–99** World History Archive / Alamy Stock Photo; **100** Naypong/Shutterstock.com; **101** © iStockphoto.com/Furchin

Chapter 7

102 Mary Terribberry/Shutterstock.com; **105** redav – Fotolia; **106** Martin Ruegner/Photographer's Choice RF/Getty Images; **107** © 2009 JupiterImages Corporation; **108** © iStock.com/grinvalds; **109** © iStockphoto.com/plherrera; **112** sunsetman/Shutterstock.com; **115** Unusual Films

Chapter 8

116 holbox/Shutterstock.com; **120–121** NASA Goddard Space Flight Center Image by Reto Stöckli (land surface, shallow water, clouds). Enhancements by Robert Simmon (ocean color, compositing, 3D globes, animation). Data and technical support: MODIS Land Group; MODIS Science Data Support Team; MODIS Atmosphere Group; MODIS Ocean Group Additional data: USGS EROS Data Center (topography); USGS Terrestrial Remote Sensing Flagstaff Field Center (Antarctica); Defense Meteorological Satellite Program (city lights); **125** Unusual Films; **126** akiyoko - Fotolia

Chapter 9

130 Martin Siepmann/Media Bakery; **134t** Life On White/Photodisc/Getty Images; **134b** © iStock.com/ollo; **135** Phil McDonald/Shutterstock.com; **136** © iStock.com/Adventure_Photo; **138** © iStockphoto.com/skodonnell; **139l** © iStockphoto.com/Bike_Maverick; **139r** © Vladimir Nenov /123RF; **140–141** BJU Photo Services; **142–143** Unusual Films

Chapter 10

146 topseller/Shutterstock.com; **150t** © iStock.com/-lvinst-; **150bl** © iStock.com/AntonioMP; **150r** R Gebbie Photography/Bigstock.com; **151** © lkordela - Fotolia.com; **152l** © iStock.com/ZavgSG; **152r** © iStock.com/mikdam; **155** Pascal Preti/Photolibrary/Getty Images; **156** © iStock.com/Christa Brunt; **157** JGI/Jamie Grill/Blend Images /Getty Images; **159** BJU Photo Services

Chapter 11

162 © iStock.com/Peter Zelei; **164** © iStock.com/sdominick; **165** © iStock.com/Christopher Futcher; **166** © iStock .com/skynesher; **168** © 2009 JupiterImages Corporation; **169t** © iStockphoto.com/jtphilips; **169b** Unusual Films; **170** Media Bakery; **171** ivonnewierink/Shutterstock.com; **173** Unusual Films; **174t, 174br** BJU Photo Services; **174bl** © 2009 JupiterImages Corporation

Chapter 12

176 Connor Walberg/The Image Bank/Getty Images; **183** © 2009 JupiterImages Corporation; **188** © JupiterImages Corporation; **189** Getty Images/Arthur Tilley; **191** Unusual Films

All maps from Map Resources